Attention and Value

attention and value

Keys to Understanding Museum Visitors

stephen bitgood

Left Coast Press Inc.

WALNUT CREEK, CA

Left Coast Press, Inc.
1630 North Main Street, #400
Walnut Creek, CA 94596
LCoastPress.com

ISBN 978-1-61132-262-0 hardback
ISBN 978-1-61132-263-7 paperback
ISBN 978-1-61132-264-4 institutional eBook
ISBN 978-1-61132-265-1 consumer eBook

Library of Congress Cataloging-in-Publication Data:
Bitgood, Stephen.
Attention and value: keys to understanding museum visitors / Stephen Bitgood.
pages cm
Includes bibliographical references and index.
ISBN 978-1-61132-262-0 (hardback : alkaline paper) —
ISBN 978-1-61132-263-7 (paperback : alkaline paper) —
ISBN 978-1-61132-264-4 (institutional ebook) —
ISBN 978-1-61132-265-1 (consumer eBook)
1. Museum visitors. 2. Attention–Social aspects. 3. Value–Social aspects. 4. Museum exhibits–Social aspects. 5. Museum exhibits–Psychological aspects. 6. Museums–Social aspects. 7. Museums–Psychological aspects. I. Title.
AM7.B567 2013
069--dc23

2013001079

Printed in the United States of America

∞™ The paper used in this publication meets the minimum requirements of American National Standard for Information Sciences—Permanence of Paper for Printed Library Materials, ANSI/NISO Z39.48–1992.

Cover design by Piper Wallis

Contents

Illustrations

Tables

Figures

PART 1

What We Know about Visitor Attention

chapter 1

Introduction

▷ **KEY IDEAS** ◁

- Visitor attention is a critical concept for scholars and museum professionals.
- Visitor attention needs to be defined in a comprehensive way using the key concepts of attention and value.
- This book uses psychology and visitor studies to explain how and where museum visitors pay attention.
- The attention-value model described in this book will help museum professionals promote engaged attention.

Key Questions about Visitor Attention

Much has been written about visitor attention, yet a comprehensive treatment of the subject still does not exist. Given the importance of this topic, both scholars and museum professionals need more careful research and reflection to understand better how attention phenomena relate to viewing exhibitions. To tackle this challenge and understand the psychological processes of attention inherent in the visitor experience, we must answer these five key questions (Bitgood, 2010):

1. **What is "visitor attention"?** What are the elements of a comprehensive definition of visitor attention? In what ways has it been defined? How has it and/or how should it be measured? How does it relate to other phenomena such as learning and fatigue?
2. **To what do visitors pay attention while viewing exhibitions?** How do visitors distribute their attention in exhibit environments? What factors are effective in capturing attention?

---

3. **Why do visitors pay attention?** What is the motivation for paying attention? What factors contribute to the motivation to pay attention or not?
4. **How do the processes or mechanisms of attention work?** Processes such as visual searching or scanning the exhibit environment, making decisions about where to focus and engage attention, and "museum fatigue" need to be understood if we are to design experiences that adequately manage visitor attention.
5. **What factors interfere with paying attention to exhibits?** How do phenomena such as "fatigue," "satiation," "competition," and "distraction" influence visitor attention, and how can these factors be minimized or eliminated?

These questions are our framework for studying visitor attention. This book answers them by describing the attention-value model of museum visitors and by exploring its implications for theory and practice.

Why Study Visitor Attention?

The key to understanding visitors in museums, zoos, science centers, and other types of exhibition centers is discovering how the processes of attention work together with the exhibition and social environments to create the museum experience. Of critical importance is understanding why, when, and how people are motivated to pay attention to exhibits and programs. In this book I focus on museum exhibitions, but the analysis can be applied to museum programs and audience research problems.

Learning is a primary concern of museum professionals, but learning is not possible until visitors' attention is focused and engaged on the objects and messages inherent in the museum experience. *Learning is a byproduct of attention.* Focusing exclusively on learning processes is putting the horse before the cart. To understand learning we must first understand attention.

A basic part of any exhibition design is a model for managing visitor attention. This model may be either explicit or implicit: it exists even if the designers are not aware of it. The model may assume that attention is primarily the product of visitor interest, knowledge, agenda, and other person[1] factors. Some may argue that visitors are capable of extracting whatever meaning they want from an exhibition relatively independent of exhibition design factors. Others argue that setting factors play the primary role in paying attention. In this book I suggest that an understanding both of person and setting, as well as their interaction, is necessary to truly understand visitor attention. Placing too much emphasis on either person or setting factors by themselves gives an incomplete understanding and is inconsistent with years of research in visitor studies and psychology.

What does it mean to "manage visitor attention"? To effectively manage attention, exhibit developers and designers must understand how attention is captured and focused, how it is motivated, and what factors impede visitors from paying attention. I believe that psychological knowledge of how attention works is fundamental to successful exhibitions.[2]

Exhibition design is both an art and a science. The best exhibitions incorporate healthy doses of both. Though artists and designers may speak to the artistic elements of exhibitions, I speak for the science of visitor studies. The science of visitor studies prevents us from the misapprehension that our exhibitions are more effective than they really are. It can help us improve the impact of our exhibitions by applying lessons learned from research. It can provide objective evidence to tell us when we are doing our job effectively and allow us to take pride in our work.

Purposes of the Book

This book has several purposes:

1. To describe a model of the visitor experience that I call the attention-value model.
2. To review research on attention and provide evidence in support of the attention-value model.
3. To offer guidelines for applying what we know about visitor attention to exhibition development and improvement.
4. To provide enough information that, if applied, will prevent your visitors from walking away muttering a line from a Rolling Stones song: "I can't get no satisfaction!"

It is my hope that, collectively, these chapters form a cohesive picture of visitor attention and offer readers tools to better manage visitor attention in museums. Most of the chapters are original writing; some are expansions of conference presentations, and a few are updated versions of previous publications. I also review relevant research on visitor attention from many other sources.

The Concept of Attention

Ashcraft and Radvansky (2010) described attention as "one of cognitive psychology's most important topics and one of our oldest puzzles." As far back as the nineteenth century, William James (1890), in what seems a very modern treatment, recognized the complexities of the concept of "attention" in his much quoted book *Principles of Psychology*:

> Everyone knows what attention is. It is the taking possession by the mind, in clear and vivid form, of one out of what seem several simultaneously possible objects or trains of thought. . . . It implies withdrawal from some things in order to deal effectively with others, and is a condition which has a real opposite in the confused, dazed, scatterbrained state which...is called "distraction" (James, 1890, p. 403).

This elegantly simple description of attention suggests that when we concentrate our attention on something we must narrow our focus on that thing and ignore other things. Thus, attention is selective; it is limited in its capacity because, in most cases, we can only seriously attend to one thing at a time; and it takes mental effort (concentration). The problem of understanding attention is very relevant to the museum experience. Viewing exhibitions is an exercise in paying attention! We must understand the psychology of visitor attention if we are to design the most effective exhibitions and programs in terms of both visitor satisfaction as well as educational impact.

Attention and Value as Organizing Concepts

The basic thesis of the attention-value model (Chapter 5) is simple: (1) at the core of exhibition success is the management of visitor attention; and (2) the primary (but not the only) motivation for paying attention is perceived value (utility or benefit divided by cost). Visitor attention can be conceived as a three-stage continuum involving *capture, focus,* and *engagement.* Learning (or any other deeply engaged experience) is an outcome of paying attention and is closely connected to the attention process rather than independent of it. Managing attention requires addressing all three stages and recognizing that each stage is influenced by a different set of factors, different mechanisms or processes, and a different set of outcome measures or indicators.

While I think that several factors play a role in what motivates visitor attention to exhibitions, *value* (defined as a ratio of utility or satisfaction or benefit divided by cost such as time, effort, or money) appears to be the most important motivator when attention is directed at something like an exhibit element. Visitors appear to compute (usually without conscious awareness) the perceived value (potential benefits divided by costs) of approaching, viewing, and engaging with an exhibit element (e.g., Bitgood, 2010; see also Chapter 5).

The result of this perceived value ratio is to pay attention (or not) to the object or element depending on how large or small the ratio of benefits to costs. Similar decision-making processes have been studied in humans and animals as documented by the literature of temporal discounting (e.g., Critchfield & Kollins, 2001; Frederick, Loewenstein, & O'Donoghue, 2002), optimal foraging theory (e.g., Rounds, 2004), and several other psychological theories. The value ratio combines personal and psychological factors (e.g., interest level in exhibit content, agenda for a particular museum visit, decision-making processes, perceptual processes, state of energy level) with environmental or setting variables (e.g., exhibit, social influence, architectural design) to predict what and how much attention will be given to exhibit elements.

Rationale for a Theoretical Model

Why do we need a theoretical model of visitor attention? A scientific theory or model helps us understand the meaning of the collective research findings. A scientific theory is not simply a wild guess; it must be consistent with the facts. More generally, a good theoretical model serves a number of important functions:

1. It provides a meaningful way to organize or make sense of the research literature. Factual information makes more sense when it is part of an interrelated conceptual framework.
2. Scientific models help explain empirical research findings in an objective, reliable, and valid way. Or, put another way, a good scientific model provides the best explanation for the facts or data available.
3. A model may allow us to make new predictions. It often provides new ways to look at an old problem. It allows connections between and among facts and phenomena that may not have been noticed before.
4. A model should be parsimonious, explaining all the known facts while invoking a minimal number of explanatory concepts.
5. A model should identify important questions relevant to phenomena under study (for example, how do visitors sequence their attention from one element to another within an exhibit display?)
6. An effective model of visitor attention should offer guidance to the exhibit developer by providing easy-to-follow principles that are easily translated to design elements.
7. A model should also provide a holistic view of visitor attention. Instead of focusing on a single stage of attention (engagement) as many viewpoints seem to do, a model should identify the steps (capture and focus of attention) leading to engagement.

8. An effective model should enumerate the relative importance of principles and variables. Since the exhibition experience includes numerous variables, it is important to understand the relevant importance of each. For example, limiting the number of words in an exhibit label is critical; however, the specific type of font used is less important as long as it can be easily read. A good model should reflect these differences in relative importance.
9. A model should provide an explanation of the psychological processes rather than simply provide a "laundry list" of variables and principles. For example, rather than list utility/satisfaction and cost as part of a list of influential variables, I have suggested that utility and cost work together as a ratio with utility as the numerator and cost as the denominator (e.g., Bitgood, 2010; Bitgood, Dukes, & Abby, 2007; see also Chapter 5).
10. A model should have social validity. That is, it should be acceptable to a large number of practitioners and other consumers of the model.

At this point it may be helpful to make a distinction between a "theory" and a "model." Both are logically deduced from empirical studies. However, there are conflicting definitions of the terms in science and economics. I take the position that "theory" involves a broad, conceptual approach, while a "model" is an "application of a theory to particular settings . . . " (Goldfarb and Ratner, 2008, p. 97). The attention-value model proposed in this book is specifically applied to visitors in museums. A more general attention-value theory may also apply to human behavior in all situations, but I am not ready at the moment to defend this position.

Framework for a Theoretical Model

To minimize misunderstandings caused by ambiguity in terminology, I will outline what I mean by a theoretical framework for visitor attention. Table 1.1 outlines my framework, which, in general, is consistent with a theoretical approach found in the science of psychology. The four headings across the top represent both measured and inferred concepts. The two concepts that can be measured are in bold, capital letters (person-setting and response-impact variables); the two inferred concepts are not in bold, and are in lowercase (explanatory mechanisms and inferred outcomes).

Person-setting factors[3]

Variables that have an impact on visitors include both person and setting factors. Their influence is indicated by changes in visitor responses (e.g., paying attention to exhibit objects). *Person* variables include a number of factors that visitors bring to the museum, including cognitive and affective processes, interests, knowledge, visit agenda, physical endurance, level of energy, and stress. *Setting* variables include both social conditions (influence of people within the visiting group, other visitors, staff) and physical conditions (exhibit design, architecture, comfort factors). Of course, person and setting variables also interact with one another, creating more complexity. For example, a visitor in a wheelchair or a small child will have a different viewing experience than a full-sized, ambulatory adult because of the differences in line of sight, and in some cases, physical accessibility to the exhibits.

Response-impact variables[4]

Response impact (changes resulting from the person-setting factors) are usually called dependent variables. These variables can be directly measured by observational data, by self-reports, and/or by recall or recognition measures of knowledge. With respect to visitor attention, observational measures include looking at, approaching, or pointing to objects; viewing time; and/or stopping at exhibit elements. They may also include "reading" (i.e., standing in front of a text label, visually focusing on the text for more than a few seconds or, alternatively, reading out loud to other group members), discussing exhibit content with other visitors, following a set of instructions in a "hands-on" or interactive exhibit, or step-by-step actions (e.g., scientific inquiry behaviors) that may infer a more complicated outcome. Self-report measures include answering questions about information that is recalled or recognized about exhibit content, discussions among group members, etc. Interviews (face-to-face surveys) and questionnaires (paper-and-pencil surveys) are both commonly used. Self-report items can be open-ended or closed-ended. They often use rating scales and other techniques designed to measure attitudes, perceptions, and feelings/affect. Direct observation and self-report measures give us different kinds of information; we cannot rely on only one type of measure to give us a complete understanding of the visitor experience.

Explanatory mechanisms

These processes are inferred from data that describe the relationship between the person-setting (independent) and response-impact (dependent) variables. These processes can be either psychological, physical, or a combination of the two. Physical processes include such things as fatigue, stress, and sensation. Psychological processes include decision-making, affect, searching, memory or knowledge acquisition, and mental fatigue. Sensory-perceptual processes are a combination of both physical and psychological. Once a process is hypothesized to explain a relationship between the person-setting and response-impact measures, further research can be conducted to test the validity of the inferred process. For example, I have suggested that interest rating and workload (amount of time and effort) influence visitor reading of text labels in an inverse relationship implied by a ratio relationship. That is, we assume that the value of the viewing experience is a function of utility such as interest level divided by workload; as workload increases (and interest level stays the same), the value ratio decreases resulting in less engaged reading.

Table 1.1: Framework for the Attention-Value Model

	PERSON-SETTING VARIABLES	Explanatory Mechanisms	RESPONSE-IMPACT VARIABLES	Inferred Outcomes
Definitions	Measurable factors that influence response-impact .	Processes that connect person-setting and response impact variables	Measures of reaction to the experience	Outcomes inferred from experience
Examples	**Personal factors:** Knowledge, interests, agenda, etc. **Setting factors:** Physical exhibits **Social influence:** family interactions	Psycho-physiological processes (searching, "fatigue," satiation, energy level, and decision-making)	Look at object Approach Choose Stop and look Read text Think about Content recall Verbal description	Learning Knowledge acquisition Restoration Inquiry Flow Immersion

Inferred outcomes

The museum world is especially interested in inferring outcomes from the museum experience. These outcomes include concepts such as understanding, learning, inquiry, flow, restoration, and simulated immersion. We assume that if individuals self-report knowing more when they exit an exhibition than when they entered, they have learned something. Unfortunately, there are many methodological problems that must be addressed when we try to make a particular inference from examining data from a museum experience. Perhaps the visitor viewing an exhibition on evolution carried a textbook on the subject and often read from it to other group members. Let's assume that the visitor group only listened to the information from the textbook and did not actually stop to view any of the exhibits. When the visitor group is interviewed after their visit, they might tell us all kinds of interesting information about evolution, but nothing from the actual exhibition. Or more realistically, the visitors might have just completed a biology course and mastered all the principles of evolution, so they did not learn anything new from their exhibition experience. The point is that we must be careful to attribute visitor measures in knowledge, attitudes, etc. to the correct cause.

The framework described here emphasizes that everyone starts with measurable events (person-setting and response-impact variables) and reasoning to deduce explanatory mechanisms and inferred outcomes. Careful analysis of our own biases and assumptions is necessary to avoid the pitfalls of faulty reasoning.

A Definition of Visitor Attention

Although the phrase "visitor attention" is commonly used in the literature (e.g., Melton, 1935; Robinson, 1928; Screven, 1999; Serrell, 1998), a comprehensive definition did not appear in the literature until recently (Bitgood, 2010). The term has been used to refer to a set of cognitive processes (e.g., Koran and Koran, 1986a). It has also referred to overt behavior: a dependent variable such as percent of visitors who stop at an exhibit display or the viewing time once stopped (Melton, 1935; Robinson, 1928; Serrell, 1998). Rarely has a distinction been made between the processes of attention such as deep engagement and the outcome measures/indicators of this process such as exhibit viewing. To develop an adequate model or theory of visitor attention, we need a more comprehensive and precise definition of "visitor attention." In this spirit, I offer the following definition:

Visitor attention is a group of psychological processes:

1. that involve a three-stage continuum (capture, focus, and engagement);
2. in which each stage is sensitive to a unique combination of variables;
3. in which actions from these processes are motivated by the interaction of person factors (personal value, interest, past experiences; perceptual, cognitive, affective, decision-making processes) and setting factors (social influence, architectural and exhibit design);
4. that are measured by multiple indicators or dependent variables (approaching an object, stopping, viewing time, reading, talking with others about, thinking about, tests of learning and memory, rating scales, etc.) with different outcome responses (indicators) at each stage.

This definition attempts to examine attention in a comprehensive manner since it incorporates all aspects of attention. Each component of the definition is expanded below:

1. **Attention as a continuum.** This suggests that the progression from capture to engagement is an interconnected continuum rather than made up of distinct phenomena. Outcomes such as learning are possible only when attention progresses from capture to engagement.
2. **Unique set of variables at each stage.** Each stage is at least partially defined by a unique combination of variables that influence the indicators of attention. For example, while the salience or power of an auditory stimulus is highly influential at the capture stage, the perceived meaning of a message is more important at the engagement stage of attention.
3. **Interaction among person and setting factors.** The definition recognizes the three general factors involved in the visitor experience. Person and setting factors are constantly working together, interacting with each other within the attention processes. This interacting framework helps to explain the motivations for paying attention. For example, visitors make decisions whether or not to pay attention based on a combination of person variables such as perceived benefit and cost, decision-making, and setting factors such as design and organization of the exhibition.
4. **Indicators of attention.** Each stage is characterized by a different set of actions or indicators. During the capture stage, actions include looking at, approaching, and stopping; during the focus stage, actions involve a narrowing of attention to a single exhibit element to the exclusion of others; and during the engagement stage, attention is characterized by highly focused examination of the exhibit content, reading text passages, discussing the content with group members, and thinking about the implications of the exhibit material.

Organization of the Book

This book is based on a large body of visitor research and evaluation studies that I have attempted to organize into a coherent theoretical model.

This chapter provides a general introduction to the problem of visitor attention. I have explained why visitor attention is important, what is meant by attention, and the criteria of a good theoretical model.

Part 1 includes four chapters all dealing with approaches to visitor attention. Chapter 2 reviews early studies (before 1940) that examined various aspects of visitor attention. The focus is on the work of Gilman (1916), Robinson (1928), Melton (1935), and Porter (1938). These studies are important both for historical background and for examining some of the issues and problems in studying visitor attention. Chapter 3 reviews theoretical viewpoints or approaches to visitor attention. Chapter 4 examines a variety of inferred outcomes of engaged attention ranging from learning to flow. Chapter 5 provides a detailed description of the attention-value model of visitors (Bitgood, 2010; 2011a). The model attempts to organize and make sense of research in both visitor studies and the literature of psychology.

Part 2 includes studies that were specifically designed to test the impact of an economical approach to value (ratio of benefit/cost). Chapters 6 and 7 describe two of our research studies that have examined the role of value (benefit divided by cost) in choosing films at a film festival and choosing to read passages of jokes and weather. In addition to providing more data on the predictive power of the value ratio, Chapter 8 describes studies that suggest two levels of engaged attention: partial and deep. Deep engagement of attention requires more mental effort and seems to require a higher value ratio.

Part 3 provides several examples of how visitor attention can be prompted. It includes others studies my colleagues and I have conducted with the goal of improving engaged attention. Attention improvement is accomplished either by increasing benefits, decreasing costs, or a combination of the two. Chapter 9 reviews studies that have prompted engaged attention with self-guides. Chapter 10 demonstrates that when individuals are prompted to engage attention by describing or comparing artwork, they read more of the text passages later. Chapter 11 compares three projects that examined the relationship between placement of exhibit labels and how much attention they receive. Chapter 12 reports a study of changes in engaged attention when text was provided that mirrored audio of attitudes toward racial integration. Finally, Chapter 13 demonstrates how the addition of life-sized cutouts of antelope species influenced how visitors engaged their attention and moved toward an exhibit overlook that they had previously ignored.

The final section (Part 4, Chapters 14–16) provides guidance on how to apply the attention-value model to the design and development of visitor experiences. Chapter 14 examines the processes associated with decreases in visitor attention: physical and mental fatigue, object competition, and object satiation. Chapter 15 focuses on how visitors navigate (orientation and circulation), and Chapter 16 provides general guidelines to managing visitor attention. A checklist provides a systematic analysis of variables that capture, focus, and engage attention (see Appendix B).

NOTES

1. I use "person" rather than "personal" to describe what visitors bring to the museum. "Person" implies both the personal history of the individual and the psychological processes of sensation, perception, and decision-making, whereas "personal" seems to imply only the former variables.
2. I consider visitor studies to be part of environmental psychology. My chapter in the *Handbook of Environmental Psychology* (Bitgood, 2002), edited by Bechtel and Churchman, is a summary of visitor studies from the viewpoint of environmental psychology.
3. "Person-setting" variables are usually called independent variables.
4. "Response-impact" variables are usually called dependent variables.

chapter 2

Early Studies In Visitor Attention

▹ **KEY IDEAS** ◃

- Early visitor studies have important lessons for us today.
- Gilman identified common design problems but others overlooked his message because of the introduction of "museum fatigue."
- Robinson and Melton's systematic studies of visitor attention provide an important foundation for what we know today and how we study visitors.
- Porter's study demonstrated how visitors distribute their attention over the course of their museum visit, but a confounding of the order of viewing and the number of exhibit cases in the galleries made her results ambiguous.

Rationale for Discussing Early Studies

The purpose of this chapter is to review studies of visitor attention conducted and published before 1940 represented by the work of Gilman (1916), Robinson (1928), Melton (1935), and Porter (1938). Each of these studies can be criticized for its conceptual, methodological, and interpretive difficulties. For example, Gilman's study was anything but an objective examination of "museum fatigue" because of his biased procedure of prompting the one participant to do whatever it takes to read exhibit labels while photos were being taken. In addition, none of these studies used survey methods in conjunction with observational methods. However, despite the limitations, the studies are still worthy of our careful examination.

The early studies are important for several reasons. First, they have historical importance: they were the first attempts to empirically study visitor attention. Second, these studies identified many of the basic concepts we use today in visitor studies; terms such as "museum fatigue," "attracting and holding

Attention and Value: Keys to Understanding Museum Visitors by Stephen Bitgood, 21–32.

power," "object satiation," "object competition," and "distraction" originated in these studies. Third, these studies illustrate some of the methodological and deductive reasoning problems associated with research on attention. Finally, these early studies provide us with a foundation for subsequent research on visitor attention.

The studies are summarized with my commentary on visitor attention as it relates to the attention-value model described in Chapter 5. These studies provide us with valuable lessons in how to study (or not study) visitor attention.

Benjamin Gilman

In his 1916 article "Museum Fatigue," Gilman (1916) coined a phrase that has captured considerable interest over the years and is often cited in the visitor literature (See Bitgood, 2009a; 2009b; 2009c). Although Gilman discussed "fatigue" as a single phenomenon, it is important to note that others have provided evidence that more than one phenomena is likely to be involved (e.g, Bitgood, 2009a; 2009b; Melton, 1935; Robinson, 1928).

Gilman was understandably concerned that poor design deprived exhibits of visitor attention. To dramatize the potential impact of poor design, he instructed one adult male to walk through an exhibition[1] and to find answers to questions that required label reading and object viewing, often under difficult conditions. His article photographically documented the physical exertion necessary to find the answers to his questions. Gilman states, "The pictures obtained indicate that an inordinate amount of physical effort is demanded of the ideal visitor by the present methods in which we offer most objects to his inspection" (Gilman, 1916, p. 252). Gilman made a questionable jump in logic by suggesting that this demonstration was evidence that poor exhibit design creates physical fatigue.

While physical exertion may play a role in "museum fatigue," it is likely to be only one of several factors that are involved in decreased attention over time. Gilman's demonstration reveals very little about "museum fatigue" for several reasons. First, he used only one individual, leaving any inference about its generality as questionable. Second, the single participant was prompted to exert himself and had to hold his position for the photographs to be taken. Third, we do not know what Gilman's subject actually experienced during the experiment; perhaps he experienced some healthy stretching that energized him for more exhibit viewing. Fourth, the Gilman report neglects other phenomena, such as "satiation" and "choice," as possible causes of "museum fatigue" (reduced attention over viewing time). Further, if prolonged physical exertion does cause exhaustion, as it seems reasonable to assume, we don't know if Gilman's subject reached the threshold of physical exhaustion in the course of his physical workout. There was no measure of decreased attention or self-reports of exhaustion. Finally, while visitors might engage in such physical exertion when prompted, uncued visitors are not likely to do so. The visitor literature suggests that visitors minimize the effort they exert, whether it is to read labels, backtrack to view additional exhibits, or mentally work through complicated ideas (see Bitgood, 2006). Gilman himself noted that visitors would not invest the effort: "Not even the hardiest sight-seer will long go through with the contortions which the pictures indicate are needed for any comprehension of much of what we display to him. After a brief initial exertion, he will resign himself to seeing practically everything imperfectly and by a passing glance" (Gilman, 1916, p. 252).

The importance of Gilman's work is that he identified some of the challenges faced by a conscientious visitor who wanted to extract as much from his/her experience as possible. Gilman also provided suggestions for improving exhibits by lowering visitors' workload when viewing exhibits. From inspection of the photographs he collected in the study, he was able to identify two sources of design problems: "(1) low installations in upright cases; and (2) broad installations in flat or desk cases." Low shelves demand bending at the knees; wide exhibit cases require bending at the hip. He argued for upright cases to stand higher and flat/desk cases to be made narrower and all cases shallower from front to back.

Ironically, Gilman did not demonstrate "museum fatigue" in his study because of faulty conclusions. His major point about designing more effective exhibits in terms of visitor time and effort seems to have been lost. However, he did stimulate additional research by Robinson and Melton, who questioned whether physical exhaustion is the cause of "museum fatigue."

Edward Robinson

Decreases in visitor attention across time in museums have often been called "museum fatigue" despite variations in conditions and outcomes involved in the situation. Edward Robinson (and his student Arthur Melton) recognized the complexity of the problem and designed studies to sort out some of the issues. As a result of these studies, it became apparent that not all decreases in visitor attention are likely to be caused by physical fatigue.

Study 1: "Museum Fatigue"

In his monograph, Robinson (1928) compared visitor attention across visitations in four different art museums of varying size and location. In addition to the observations in the four museums, Robinson conducted a laboratory study with students who were exposed to 100 art prints to examine while seated at a table. The students controlled how long they looked at each print, but since they were seated, did not experience the physical fatigue of visitors who walked through the museums. See Table 2.1 for a comparison of number of paintings, size of museum, and average view time.

Since the number of artworks actually viewed by individuals varied considerably both within each museum and among the four museums, Robinson divided the total number of artworks that each visitor viewed into successive tenths. Thus, if a visitor only viewed 10 paintings, each painting counted one-tenth. If a visitor viewed 100 artworks, then each 10 paintings were included in each tenth. Using this method, Robinson was able to compare visitor behavior across different portions of their museum visit even though visitors viewed a different number of pictures.

In Robinson's study, individuals varied in how many artworks they viewed. This variation points to an important factor Robinson did not explicitly discuss. In the museum, individuals chose to view or not to view artworks as they passed them by. In the laboratory, however, the participants' only choice was how long they viewed, not whether or not they viewed a work of art.

RESULTS. Table 2.1 summarizes the findings. There was a tendency for the in-museum visitors to spend fewer seconds per painting over successive tenths of viewing. The laboratory participants, although they viewed each artwork longer than the museum visitors, still showed a decline in attention despite the lack of physical exertion. In all groups, visitors who viewed a larger number of artworks did not show any difference in the rate of decline when compared with visitors who viewed a smaller number. Thus, rate of decline (difference from highest to lowest average viewing time over successive artwork) was not a function of the total number of pictures viewed.

Robinson recognized that there is no one simple explanation for these results, and that comparing the museum visitors and laboratory participants is fraught with methodological difficulties. Despite the difficulties, it seems reasonable to conclude that decreases in viewing time across visitation is not due to physical "fatigue" or exhaustion because: (1) visitors at the small museums showed the same decreased attention over time than those at the large museum; (2) visitors who viewed a smaller number of artworks showed the same rate of decreased attention than those who viewed a larger number; and (3) the laboratory subjects showed a similar rate of decreased attention than the actual museum visitors despite the lack of physical exertion from sitting at a table.

It is difficult to assess what impact the choice of viewing each artwork had on Robinson's findings. The actual museum visitors could choose whether or

Table 2.1: Viewing Time During Each Tenth of Viewing Art (From Robinson 1928)

	Lab Ss	Museum 1	Museum 2	Museum 3	Museum 4
Paintings	100 s	1,000 s	150 s	140 s	154–256 s
Galleries	—	40 s	6 s	6 s	ND
Average	—	25 min	17 min	17 min	15 min
	View Time for each Tenth, seconds				
First	26.0	10.8	15.0	14.8	7.1
Second	27.9	9.7	11.3	12.9	7.5
Third	28.1	10.1	10.8	17.0	8.5
Fourth	26.0	9.2	10.9	16.1	8.7
Fifth	25.7	9.0	9.9	18.3	7.8
Sixth	25.3	9.4	11.4	14.3	8.5
Seventh	25.7	8.0	11.8	12.9	7.8
Eighth	22.9	8.5	12.6	11.7	7.0
Ninth	22.2	9.7	10.4	11.0	8.9
Tenth	19.3	9.9	12.2	14.5	6.9

Ss indicates participants, ND, no data.

not to attend to each piece of artwork, while the laboratory subjects could not. This might account for some of the differences between the laboratory subjects and the museum visitors.

Study 2: Object Competition

Robinson's next study was an experimental examination of how object competition ("isolation" in his words) influences attention to artworks in a laboratory study. Robinson presented either one, two, or ten art prints at a time to participants who were seated at a table. The procedure was similar to the laboratory study in the first study. All participants viewed a total of 100 black-and-white prints. The participants were instructed to examine each print for as long as they desired. In the two-at-a-time scenario, a total of 50 trials were given; for the ten-at-a-time scenario, ten trials were given.

RESULTS. The average viewing time per artwork (Table 2.2) was longer when one print was presented at a time than for presentation of either two or ten prints at a time. The rate of decrement of viewing time across successive tenths was about the same no matter how many prints were presented each time. Finally, a warm-up effect was observed for all groups: the longest viewing time occurred on the third or fourth interval.

It is not clear if the longer viewing time for a single print than for two or ten prints is due to distraction or some other mechanism. When more than one object is presented at the same time, the workload per trial is higher, which may discourage viewing more than one print carefully.

Table 2.2: Viewing Time for Each Condition (from Robinson 1928)

Sets of Prints	Viewing Time, seconds		
	One at a time	Two at a time	Ten at a time
1–20	26.9	24.1	17.0
21–40	27.0	23.7	19.6
41–60	25.5	21.8	19.0
61–80	23.4	17.5	16.0
81–100	20.6	14.9	13.8

Study 3: Variety of Artwork Types

Robinson's next study addressed the possibility that the variety of picture content was important in producing "museum fatigue." He presented a total of 25 prints, five at a time. The samples included five prints of each of the following types: landscapes, Madonnas, portraits, "marines" (as Robinson called them), and animals.

Study Conditions

Five prints of the first type were presented in the first trial; five prints of the second type were presented in the second trial; etc.

1. Two types of content were presented in each trial.
2. Three types of content were presented in each trial.
3. Four types of content were presented in each trial.
4. Five types of content were presented in each trial.

RESULTS. As shown in Table 2.3, an increase from 15 to 20 seconds occurred from the first to the fourth condition. However, condition 5 showed a decrease in viewing time.

What are the implications of this study? Variety appeared to increase attention (viewing time) up to a point (four different types), but five different types at a time erased the advantage of variety. "Variety" may be a misleading concept in this study since all subjects viewed all of the same artwork. The difference between groups was in terms of whether the variety was within or between trials. In the first condition (one type per card), the variety was between trials, since each trial had a different set of similar cards (e.g., all Madonnas followed by all portraits, followed by all marines, followed by all animals). In the fifth condition (five types per card), variety was all within trials since each card had one of each type. Thus, similar objects presented close together appears to result in decreased attention rather than variety itself. If this is the case, decreased attention in the one-type-per-card condition seemed to result in object satiation (repetitive homogenous stimulation presented over a short time period) compared with the conditions that included three or four types per card. It is not clear why the five-types-per-card condition resulted in decreased attention. Perhaps too much variety introduces another factor: perceptual distraction.

Table 2.3: Viewing Time per Art Print for Each Condition (from Robinson, 1928)

Condition	Average Viewing Time, seconds
One type/card	14.6
Two types/card	17.2
Three types/card	18.3
Four types/card	19.8
Five types/card	15.5

Study 4: Use of Pamphlets to Reduce "Fatigue"

Since the decreases in attention over time in the first study were probably due to object satiation rather than physical fatigue or exhaustion, Robinson attempted to find a way to maintain attention over the entire visit. He compared the use of a pamphlet (visitor guide) to no pamphlet in Small Museum 2 to assess its impact on "museum fatigue" or the decreased attention over time. The pamphlet focused on 20 of the artworks that were installed in the museum. The location, title, and a brief description of these artworks were provided.

More than 60 percent (55 of 86) used the pamphlet effectively. Of those who did not use it, 24 carried it but did not look at it, four looked at it as they left the museum, and two initially looked at it but did not use it.

RESULTS. Those who used the pamphlet spent more time in the museum (28 versus 17 minutes). In addition, they viewed a larger percentage of artworks (46 versus 30 percent). Those who did not use the pamphlet showed the usual decreased attention (viewing time) as they proceeded through the museum. Those who used the pamphlets actually showed an increased in average viewing time across successive tenths of the visit. The pamphlet appeared to counteract the "fatigue" effect usually observed with visitors. As indicated by other studies (see Chapter 11), visitor guides or handouts do help increase or maintain visitor attention to exhibits.

Arthur Melton

Arthur Melton (1935), one of Robinson's students, expanded Robinson's work on visitor attention. Some of his pioneering findings included how visitors circulate through exhibition spaces, the attracting power of exits within an exhibit gallery, turning at intersections, and the impact of object competition (see Bitgood, 2006). In this review, we include only three studies that relate to decrements in attention across successive exhibit viewing in museums.

In one of Melton's studies, he varied the number of paintings in a gallery from 6 to 36, in increments of 6. The purpose of this study was to assess the influence of "competition" or "gallery density" (number of paintings in the gallery). The original six paintings were distributed along the four walls and, in subsequent conditions, additional paintings were added in positions around the original six. As the number of paintings increased, the percentage of stops at paintings (number of stops per number of paintings) decreased systematically. However, once stopped, the average viewing time per painting remained constant. Increased "competition" or "density" (number of paintings) appeared to influence the attracting power (percentage of stops), but not the viewing time. Melton argued that every painting competes for attention with every other painting. Adding new paintings has a "distracting" effect on visitors, which results in decreased viewing. Note that decrements in viewing time or attention that results from "competition" should be considered distinct from decrements produced by "museum fatigue" phenomena (exhaustion, satiation, etc.). The defining conditions for "competition" do not require viewing over successive exhibit elements. However, "choice" may be the mechanism that is shared by both "competition" and "museum fatigue." Visitors may choose to view fewer artworks or view for a shorter time period either because there are so many available, because they become satiated after viewing too many, or because they suffer from some type of exhaustion.

As discussed in this chapter, "competition" occurs when there are simultaneous competing stimuli; "satiation" occurs as the artwork is being consumed (viewed). Melton argued that every object competes for attention with every other object, implying that each additional object is a potential competitor distractor from the target object. This hypothesis might be called "selection by distraction." However, my colleagues and I suggested in a 2008 conference paper (Bitgood, McKerchar, & Dukes, 2012) that the decreased attention to stimulus competition in this study might have been caused more by selection based on choice (visitors select a smaller percentage of paintings at which to stop as the total number available increases). Selection by choice may be important in understanding "museum fatigue" phenomena as well as stimulus competition. In the case of "museum fatigue" (physical or mental tiredness), visitors may become more selective to avoid a state of physical or mental fatigue/tiredness. (See Chapter 15 for an additional discussion.)

In a related study of competition and satiation, Melton manipulated the number of artworks in a gallery in the following way. The gallery was divided into 12 sections. For all conditions, the first section always had 12 paintings. The remaining 11 sections varied: 4 artworks per section in the first condition; 8 artworks per section in the second condition; and 12 artworks per section the third condition. Table 2.4 summarizes the findings. The decrease in viewing time across sections was greater for the 4- and 8-painting conditions than it was in the 12-painting condition. Satiation (decreased attention across successive paintings) was not found in the 12-painting condition, but this condition had the shortest viewing time across all conditions. The percentage of paintings actually viewed decreased dramatically between the 4-painting, 8-painting, and 12-painting conditions, although the absolute number viewed changed from 4.5, to 7.4, and finally to 6.8, in the 12-painting condition.

Table 2.4: Average Viewing Time per Exhibit Section (from Melton, 1935)

	Viewing Time per Section, seconds		
	4 paintings	8 paintings	12 paintings
Sections 1–2	7.9	6.7	5.1
Sections 10–11	7.0	5.0	5.2
Percentage Viewed	56.5	45.9	6.8
No. Viewed	4.5	7.4	6.8

The density of paintings (4 versus 8 versus 12 per section) had a marked impact on average viewing time per painting. The higher the density, the shorter the viewing time and the smaller the percentage of artworks viewed. Decreases in viewing time over successive artworks viewed did not occur for the 12-painting condition. Higher density resulted in greater visitor selectivity in what they viewed: the highest percentage of the total available was viewed when there was the lowest density (four per section).

Mildred Porter

Mildred Porter (1938), another of Robinson's students, published her dissertation work in still another American Association of Museums (AAM; now American Alliance of Museums) monograph. She tracked visitors through the Peabody Museum of Natural History at Yale University, recording the circulation pathway, where visitors stopped, and the duration of stops.

RESULTS. Porter found a decrease in attention as visitors viewed successive galleries. Although the order of exhibit gallery viewing did predict viewing time per case, a confounding variable (number of cases per gallery) might also account for the decreased attention since the number of cases increased across galleries. Number of cases per gallery might cause competition much like making additional objects available did in the Robinson and Melton studies. The decreased viewing time per case across successive viewing could be the result of satiation, competition, or both.

In a second study, Porter compared a guided group (visitors given a handout or leaflet) with an unguided group. Tables 2.5 and 2.6 show the results. The handouts (leaflets) increased attention to exhibits, but a decrease in attention per exhibit area across time was evident, although the percentage of stops remained higher than in the no-leaflet group. For both guided and unguided visitors, there was a strong relationship between the number of cases per gallery and visitor attention. The confounding of density (number of cases per gallery) and order of viewing make it difficult to draw any strong conclusions as to whether the results were due to competition (as in the Melton study of gallery density) or satiation. However, since the two mammal galleries had about the same number of cases (31 and 30), but were viewed in a different order, we should have some idea about which phenomenon was most important. A satiation effect would predict higher attention to the first mammal gallery, while a competition effect would predict the same attention to each mammal gallery because of similar density. The similarity in the percentage of stops at these two galleries favors a competition interpretation: the higher the density (i.e., the more exhibit elements), the greater the competition for attention of each element.

Table 2.5: Percentage of Visitors Who Stopped in Each Section (from Porter, 1938)

Viewing Order	No. of Cases	Leaflet, %	No Leaflet, %
1	22	61	46
2	31	39	30
3	30	40	30
4	48	29	21
5	56	19	12

Table 2.6 indicates that the leaflet also influenced interpretive text reading. Visitors with the leaflet read more than those with no leaflet until the very last exhibition area (section 5), although there was a steady decline as the museum visit progressed. Note that the two mammal areas were again similar in terms of visitor response, despite the order of viewing.

Table 2.6: Percentage of Visitors Reading Labels in Each Section (from Porter, 1938)

View Order	No. of Cases	Leaflet, %	No Leaflet, %
1	22	36	22
2	31	24	12
3	30	20	12
4	48	17	10
5	56	10	10

Although Porter interpreted her findings in terms of exhibition viewing order, the evidence suggests that the number of exhibit elements per exhibit area might have been more important. Given the confounding variables, we can only speculate about the outcome. However, we can clearly argue that the leaflet helped maintain attention across the visit, although not to the extent that was reported in Robinson's fourth study described earlier in this chapter.

There is still another interpretation problem with Porter's study. Given the self-selecting nature of leaflet use, those who used leaflets were probably more likely to read labels since reading is associated with using the leaflets.

General Discussion

How should we place these early studies in proper perspective? In retrospect, we could label these attempts as naive. Gilman's concern over poorly designed exhibits was expressed in terms of "fatigue" rather than the cost (time and effort) required to engage with the exhibits. Robinson and Melton did not recognize how important choice might be in the visitor experience. Porter confounded the order of viewing with the number of exhibit cases per gallery. Note that at that time (early twentieth century), because of the strong influence of radical behaviorism in academic psychology, Robinson, Melton, and Porter did not use self-report data to assess knowledge acquisition, attitude change, or degree of satisfaction with the visitor experience. Psychology became more open to multiple methods under the influence of functionalism (e.g., William James, John Dewey, G. Stanley Hall).

Despite the shortcomings, these studies have provided an important starting point for understanding visitor attention. They identified many of the problems that we still wrestle with today. The findings from these studies reveal some important results that shaped subsequent research:

1. The studies found that decreases in attention across viewing time occur consistently.
2. These decreases in attention across time are apparently usually not due to physical exertion.
3. Object competition is one factor that results in decreased attention. The higher the density of objects, the more competition for attention and the lower the percentage of objects that will be given attention.
4. Object satiation is another well-documented phenomenon. Visitor attention over successive exhibit viewing decreases because of a short-term loss of attention from experiencing too much of a good thing too quickly.

While this chapter focuses on empirical studies (at least those prior to 1940), the next chapter describes the variety of theoretical approaches that have arisen over the years to explain the results of visitor research and evaluation studies.

NOTE

1. In this book I distinguish between "exhibit" (a single display) and "exhibition" (a collection of physically related exhibits with a common theme).

chapter 3

Review of Visitor Attention Theories and Models

▹ **KEY IDEAS** ◃

- There have been many approaches to the concept of visitor attention.
- A representative sample of approaches is briefly examined using the criteria of Chapter 1 for assessing theories of attention.
- While there is a diversity of theories and models of visitor attention, many are not expressed as theories of visitor attention.
- The approaches described in this chapter provide an excellent beginning for developing a model of visitor attention.

Introduction

Chapter 2 reported the results of early studies, but did not provide detailed, systematic theoretical explanations for the results. The important considerations with any theory are: How effectively does the theory explain the facts? Does the theory make sense of the domain knowledge so that it furthers understanding? Does the theory identify new questions that need to be answered? Can the theory be tested by data and possibly proven wrong? How powerful is the theory in predicting outcomes? Does the theory tell us how all the important concepts are organized into a logical framework? Does the theory invoke a minimum of concepts (i.e., is it parsimonious)?

Criteria for Assessing Theories/Models of Attention

In Chapter 1, visitor attention is defined in terms of five elements. Chapter 2 described and critiqued the early studies of visitor attention. This chapter offers brief descriptions of various theoretical approaches to/viewpoints of visitor attention. Since it would be difficult to include every viewpoint written

Attention and Value: Keys to Understanding Museum Visitors by Stephen Bitgood, 33–53.

about attention, an attempt is made to choose sources that are both prominent and representative of how visitor attention has been discussed in the literature. For comparative purposes, each viewpoint is briefly described in terms of the five elements of the definition of attention in Chapter 1 and a general critique of the viewpoint is made. To refresh the reader's memory, the five elements are:

1. **Attention as a continuum.** Does the theory/model recognize a progression of attention from a shallow, unfocused state to a highly focused and deeply engaged state? In other words, does the approach recognize the importance of capturing attention as well as engaging attention?
2. **Response-impact measures of attention.** What measures or indicators of attention does the theory/model identify? Does it include measures of attention capture such as approach and stop? Does it include measures of focus and engagement such as viewing time, reading text material, discussing exhibit content with other group members, physically interacting with exhibit objects/devices, and measures of knowledge and/or skills? Are the response measures clearly distinguished from inferred outcomes and explanatory mechanisms?
3. **Person-setting variables.** What factors or variables does the theory/model invoke as influencing visitor attention? Does the theory include: (1) person or visitor variables; (2) variables associated with the physical and social setting, and (3) the interaction between person and setting variables? Or does it focus on a limited set of variables (e.g., person variables such as agenda, or setting variables such as geometric sight lines)?
4. **Explanatory mechanisms.** What are the processes that explain the relationship between response indicators/measures and variables that influence attention (person-setting factors)? Are the mechanisms consistent with the literature in psychology? Do they include factors that motivated visitors to attend? Do they include phenomena that result in decreased attention to exhibit material?
5. **Inferred outcomes.** What final outcomes are inferred from the evidence and assumed to be important? Outcomes include such phenomena as learning, scientific inquiry, psychological flow, immersion, and restoration.

In addition to these five definitional elements, this chapter includes a general critique of each viewpoint. Those whose viewpoints are being critiqued may not agree with the definitional criteria offered in this book. However, the criteria were developed from a review of both the visitor studies and the psychology literatures. Note also that many of these viewpoints discussed in this chapter do not use the term "attention" to signify the processes and variables identified in the first chapter despite the fact that they clearly encompass the concept of attention used in this book.

Edward Robinson and Arthur Melton

As reported in Chapter 2, Edward Robinson (1928) and Arthur Melton (1935) conducted the first systematic, psychological studies of visitor behavior. Both of their AAM monographs have become classics in visitor studies and the museum world in general. While they did not propose a formal theory of visitor attention, they offered a number of basic principles from which an implied theory can be deduced.

1. **Continuum of attention.** Robinson and Melton did not explicitly divide attention into stages. However, at least partial recognition of multiple stages is implied by the use of percentages of stopping (capture) and viewing time (focus/engagement) as measures of visitor impact.
2. **Response-impact measures.** Two measures of attention were most often used in the Robinson-Melton studies. Percentages of stopping and viewing time were obtained in actual museum studies and viewing time alone in Robinson's simulated studies (1928). They also reported text reading in one of the studies, but reading was not consistently reported.[1]
3. **Person-setting variables.** Robinson and Melton studied variables such as size, number, variety, and placement/location of artwork in exhibit halls. In addition, they examined the influence of open doors within an exhibit hall and amount and type of exhibit object exposure (e.g., number of paintings in the museum and exhibit hall). Person variables were rarely discussed other than to control the collection of visitor samples. These studies convincingly document the importance of physical setting factors.

Setting variables are correlated with response-impact measures (indicators) to provide empirical principles (e.g., "large objects capture more attention than small ones"). To explain these principles, we must turn to the theoretical mechanisms or processes that might be involved.

4. **Explanatory mechanisms.** Robinson and Melton identified several processes or mechanisms associated with attention.
   a. **Salience of objects.** Some objects have strong attraction by nature of their size, by their placement within an exhibit hall, or by being isolated from other objects.

b. **Distraction/competition.** Robinson and Melton argued that every object in an exhibit hall competes for attention with every other object. They assumed competition resulted in perceptual distraction, where the visual presence of any object other than the target serves as a perceptual distraction, resulting in decreased attention to exhibit elements. Melton did not speculate on the nature of perceptual distraction. It is possible that automatic visual scanning occurs when more than one object is available at a time. Such scanning might then decrease attention to a target exhibit element because of limited capacity to attend, resulting in distraction from a target object.

c. **Object satiation.** Robinson and Melton believed that what is usually called "museum fatigue" is primarily the result of object satiation (decrease in attention resulting from repeated presentation of homogonous exhibit content). Satiation can be considered boredom resulting from the monotony of stimulation by similar objects. Robinson and Melton did recognize that multiple factors, in addition to object satiation, might contribute to "fatigue-like" phenomena.

d. **Movement patterns.** Melton found that when entering a symmetrical exhibit hall with no strong attractor pulling visitors in one direction or another, visitors have a strong tendency to turn right when entering the hall, circulate in a counterclockwise direction, and exit from the hall if and when encountering an open door. Thus, objects at the end of a circulation route within an exhibit hall tend to receive very little attention since more and more visitors drop off from the route as they proceed through the gallery. Melton also described the "exit gradient" as the tendency to walk in a straight line from the entrance to the exit of the exhibit hall and to pay less attention to objects when approaching the exit.

5. **Inferred outcomes.** Robinson and Melton considered "attention" equivalent to "interest." There was no discussion of why these terms should have identical meanings. Since these researchers did not use self-report measures, perhaps they did not consider the possibility of measuring "interest" with self-report measures to distinguish it from the observational measures of percentages of stopping and viewing time. The psychology literature of the time did not make a clear distinction between attention and interest, and the Robinson-Melton approach seems to reflect the thinking of the time. The only discussion of learning was in the school group study (Melton, Feldman, & Mason, 1936).

Summary and Critique

Robinson and Melton conducted a number of studies that examined how percentages of visitor stopping and viewing time relate to setting factors within the exhibition. Their research provided a number of findings that are still relevant today. However, they restricted their efforts primarily to only two measures: percentages of stops and viewing time. They did not consider the range of other possible measures of attention often used today. They explained object competition as the result of perceptual distraction, but did not consider the possibility that visitors become increasingly selective in what they pay attention to when faced with increased alternative choices (Bitgood, McKerchar, & Dukes, 2012).

Although they provided a solid foundation for future research, they did not address how visitors become deeply engaged with exhibit content. Melton reported several studies of movement or circulation patterns through exhibit halls, and did not always find that visitors turned right (although some recent authors report the right-turning bias as a given fact). Recent studies suggest that people turn right only if it requires fewer steps or less time and effort rather than a general bias to turn right (see Chapter 16 and Bitgood, 2006).

Finally, Robinson and Melton did not make a distinction between "attention" and "interest." While the two are obviously related, if we are to objectively study these phenomena, we must be precise in our definitions. Logically, it is possible to have an interest in some topic, but not attend to exhibit content because either the visitor did not detect or notice the exhibit, or the exhibit elements were presented in a way that appeared to require too much time and effort (e.g., long text labels). Thus, these concepts should be carefully defined to indicate that one can have interest without attention. It is also possible to have attention without interest.

Harris Shettel

Harris Shettel published a number of important visitor-related articles beginning in the 1960s. In addition to his scholarly contributions, he was professionally active in the American Alliance of Museums' Committee on Audience Research & Evaluation (serving as Chair) and the Visitor Studies Association (serving as President). He was co-editor with Chan Screven of the *ILVS Review: A Journal of Visitor Behavior*. As an evaluator and researcher, he has persistently emphasized goal-referenced objectives both in guiding exhibition development and as a basis upon which exhibition effectiveness should be evaluated. He was the first to use exhibit mock-ups to pretest the effectiveness of exhibit elements in communicating with intended visitors (now known as formative evaluation) (Shettel, et al., 1968, pp. 94–110).

1. **Continuum of attention.** Shettel and his colleagues (Shettel, et al., 1968) recognized the continuum of attention by proposing a three-stage process: initially attracting visitors to the exhibit (attracting power), maintaining attraction (holding power), and optimizing relevant learning (learning power). "If an exhibit is weak in any of these three areas, the chances of its achieving its stated objectives would appear to be greatly lessened" (p. 153).
2. **Response-impact measures.** Shettel proposed three measures to correspond to the three levels of attention: attraction (percentage of visitors within viewing range who stop), holding power ratio (average viewing time divided by average time it takes to actually view/use all of the exhibit elements), and learning (measure of recall and recognition of exhibit content). Shettel proposed that holding power be expressed as a ratio of average viewing time of noncued visitors divided by average viewing time of a few individuals who were instructed to thoroughly examine all exhibit elements. Since exhibit elements differ widely in terms of size and complexity, the Shettel's proposed holding power calculation allows cross-exhibit viewing time comparisons to be made on an equitable basis.
3. **Person-setting variables.** Shettel did not explicitly identify important variables at each stage of attention. However, he did categorize relevant variables into three areas: visitor, exhibit design, and exhibit effectiveness.
   a. **Visitor variables:** age/educational level, sex, knowledge background, socioeconomic level, extent to which viewing is voluntary, and interest level.
   b. **Exhibit design variables:** amount of text material, readability level, legibility of text material, use of audiovisual devices, total amount of time required to view exhibit materials, internal location and sequence of display elements, and use of "constant" (static) and "dynamic" models.
   c. **Exhibit effectiveness variables:** ability to attract attention, holding power, ability to bring about a change in level of open-ended conceptual knowledge (recall), change in level of open-ended factual knowledge (recognition), and changes in level of exhibit-specific knowledge.
4. **Explanatory mechanisms.** Rather than study the processes or mechanisms involved in attention, Shettel focused on goal-referenced learning as an outcome. Consistent with most visitor literature, learning was considered the major product of engaged attention. While he also recognized the importance of capturing and focusing visitor attention as a prerequi-

site to learning, he had not addressed the specific mechanisms of attention, but has nevertheless recognized that these psychological processes are important.

5. **Inferred outcomes.** Shettel focused on learning as the major outcome of concern for exhibitions.

Summary and Critique

Shettel was one of the first to recognize the importance of viewing attention as a continuum, arguing for three measures appropriate for the three stages of attention (attracting power for capture, viewing time for focus, and learning assessment for engagement). While he did not extensively study the processes that connect response-impact variables with the person-setting variables, he did provide categories for organizing these variables. His organizing framework of categories related to visitor attention (visitor, exhibit design, and exhibit effectiveness variables) is, in many ways, similar to the later approaches of Lakota (1975) and Koran and Koran (1986a). The distinction between "exhibit design" and "exhibit effectiveness" variables is unclear since variables contained in each category overlap ("ability to attract attention," etc.); the categories are not mutually exclusive. While emphasizing the importance of learning, Shettel is less interested in examining the mechanisms or processes that tie the person-setting variables (e.g., agenda and exhibit design factors) to the response indicators of attention. He has consistently emphasized the importance of explicitly stated objectives to guide exhibit design and evaluation.

Bob Lakota

Bob Lakota (a.k.a. Raye Newmann) developed his approach to visitor attention while at the Smithsonian Institution in the 1970s. Lakota's model was based on a complex methodology and statistical analysis. His was a global assessment of exhibition success rather than a framework that would allow assessment of individual exhibit elements. Given the space limitation, I will describe only his attraction power model (percentage of individuals who visit an exhibit hall) here, since his holding power and effectiveness outcome model uses the same logical approach and follows Shettel's model.

1. **Continuum of attention.** Lakota (1975) offered a "visitor interaction rating scale" that included five levels:
    a. **Passing through:** walking through the exhibit hall with little or no attention to exhibit elements.

b. **Scanning or surveying:** checking out the hall, attempting to get a comprehensive view, but not engaging with exhibit elements.

c. **Browsing:** casual viewing with occasional stops, or "unfocused looking."

d. **Partial engagement:** stopping to look at exhibit elements, but attention is divided; selects only one or two items to view within an exhibition; stopping to look from a distance.

e. **Full engagement:** close examination of exhibits, including reading and studying the content, and engaging in behaviors that suggest deeper mental processing of the exhibit content.

2. **Response-impact measures.** Following Shettel, Lakota identified three measures of effectiveness: attracting power (percentage of individuals who visit the hall), holding power (average viewing time), and effectiveness outcomes (measurable changes in learning, attitudes, etc.). For each criteria, Lakota computed an additive model of success that required multiple factors (visitor tracking through the exhibition, visitor recognition tasks of exhibit content using either photographs or written descriptive text, and ratings of exhibit characteristics by museum professionals).

3. **Person-setting variables.** As noted earlier in this chapter, Lakota's criteria for success were computed from a combination of data: visitor tracking, visitor response to photographs and text passages of exhibit hall content, and ratings of exhibit hall characteristics from knowledgeable professionals. The variables involved in each of the four components of success (for attraction) are listed below:

a. **Accessibility.** This measure included order of visitation taken from visitor tracking data as well as the proximity of the exhibit hall to entrances, stairways, and elevators.

b. **Content.** This criterion was derived from a combination of interest, familiarity, awareness, desire, and expectancy taken from the recognition-sorting tasks using photography of elements from exhibit halls (picture recognition) and brief, written explanations of hall content (card recognition).

c. **Design.** Three museum staff members rated exhibit halls using five design variables (conceptual organization, spaciousness, extensiveness, new display, and instructional content).

d. **Socioecology.** This criterion included noise decibel reading, crowd density ratings around displays, and ratings of the proportion of children to adults in hall sectors.

4. **Explanatory mechanisms.** Lakota proposed an additive model of attention in which the derived measures (accessibility, content, design, and

socioecological factors) combine to give an overall level of attention. Lakota's statistical/mathematical approach requires considerable time, effort, and knowledge of statistics. Additional research is needed to establish the merits of this approach.

5. **Inferred outcomes.** Lakota, like Shettel, focused on learning as an outcome. Learning was inferred by measuring visitor recognition of photographs and text descriptions of exhibit content.

Summary and Critique

Lakota collected multiple measures of attention, combined them into general concepts based on statistical analysis, and tested a simple additive statistical model. Since his model defined success in terms of global exhibit hall attention, it does not provide a diagnostic analysis for individual elements within exhibitions. On the plus side, he did develop three models appropriate for each of the three stages of attention identified in Chapter 1.

Unfortunately, no one has followed up on Lakota's methodology and findings. The Smithsonian Institution museums may be unique in terms of who visits and how often, so it is difficult to know how much his findings generalize to other museums. Since no other studies have used his "visitor interaction rating scale," it is difficult to know if it has good reliability (inter-rater consistency) or generality to other museums.

He was the first to use sophisticated statistical analysis of visitor-impact measures, but his complex analysis might be intimidating to museum professionals who are not familiar with statistical methods and mathematical models. His use of photographs and written descriptions of exhibit content was a clever way to assess recognition of exhibit content and a more sensitive measure of learning than recall.

Chan Screven

In the last four decades of the twentieth century, Chandler Screven contributed a volume of research studies, literature reviews, and a number of guiding principles related to visitor attention (e.g., Screven, 1976, 1986, 1992, 1999). He also provided an annotated bibliography and a journal related to visitor studies. In his last major publication, Screven (1999) reviewed a large body of educational and psychological literature, described a complex view of "information design in informal settings," and offered a number of principles relevant to designing exhibitions. His chapter is less accessible to museum professionals because it is published outside the museum publication arena; however, it provides a wealth of information and principles on visitor attention.

Both "attention" and "communication" are central to his view of information design. *Attention* "includes various processes involved in detecting, interpreting, and acting on existing schemas and new incoming information." (Screven, 1999, p. 143). *Communication,* on the other hand, "describes the overall impact of these [attention] processes" (p. 143).

1. **Continuum of attention.** Screven recognized the importance of a continuum of attention, repeatedly emphasizing that attention must first be captured and engaged as part of the learning process. However, his writing tended to focus on learning and the engagement of attention.
2. **Response-impact measures.** Screven argued for multiple measures of attention. He noted that percentages of stopping and viewing time tell us little about a visitor's degree of involvement. He emphasized the quality of attention (active-passive, focused-unfocused) at each exhibit element, making his approach more diagnostic than Lakota's. He showed more concern than other researchers for the mechanisms or processes of attention, with many citations from the psychological and educational literature. He recognized that gross measures of attention give little information about what is coded in memory, how information is interpreted, or how it is related to the individual's existing knowledge. He also recognized that selective attention is required to communicate the message, thus recognizing the importance of focusing attention. The following statement indicates his appreciation for the complexity of attention processes: "Attention varies in how long it is sustained, how efficiently it scans exhibit content, how well it separates meaningful from peripheral data and focuses on interrelationships among information elements" (Screven, 1999, p. 143).
3. **Person-setting variables.** Perhaps more than other researchers, Screven was aware of the complexity of attention processes, citing numerous factors that might influence attention. He noted that exhibit content must have personal value to visitors to engage visitor attention. He also recognized the importance of exhibit design variables. If the design does communicate the exhibit's message quickly to the visitor, it is likely to be ignored. According to Screven, variables that influence "efficiency" include lighting, text legibility, crowding, sight lines, terminology, and visual overload.
4. **Explanatory mechanisms.** Screven suggested that attention processes have three elements: (1) the information field, (2) perceptual filters, and (3) exhibit efficiency. The *information field* includes all the information elements that make up a given message. *Perceptual filters* originate from

prior knowledge, attitudes, preconceptions, and beliefs. Filters interpret and often distort the meaning of exhibit content. *Exhibit efficiency* is the time and effort it takes to process a display's content. Effective exhibits must be processed quickly if they are to communicate their messages.

Summary and Critique

Screven included most of the elements identified by our definition of visitor attention. He provided an excellent review of the educational and psychological literature that must be considered in formulating a theory of visitor attention. His concept of "exhibit efficiency" is particularly noteworthy since it emphasizes the importance of time and effort required to process exhibit information. The major limitation of his approach is that it lacks a parsimonious network of principles and deductions that are logically tied together. However, the principles Screven identified must be part of any adequate theory or model of attention. It is unclear how "perceptual filters" are distinct from the "information field" and "exhibit efficiency" since efficiency would seem to be determined by the interaction between the information field and the perceptual filters (psychological processes of attention). Unfortunately, no formula for measuring exhibit efficiency is provided.

John Koran

John Koran and his colleagues at the University of Florida have contributed an important body of work related to visitor attention (e.g., Koran & Koran, 1983, 1986a, 1986b, 1988; Koran, Koran, & Foster, 1989). Unfortunately, John's sudden death from a heart attack ended his important work. Although Koran's viewpoint is more cognitive, it shares some similarity to Shettel's in that the variables are organized into three major categories.

1. **Continuum of attention.** Koran did not explicitly recognize a continuum of three stages of attention. As did several other researchers, he focused on the engagement stage rather than expanding on the capture and focus phases of the continuum.
2. **Response-impact measures.** I am somewhat confused about which measures and concepts are placed in which category in the Koran framework. In at least one study (Koran, Koran, & Foster, 1989), "attention" was defined as viewing time and learning as an outcome. In other publications (Koran & Koran, 1983, 1986a), desired outcomes included knowledge, curiosity, and motivation. Making "learning" and "knowledge" equivalent concepts seems to solve the discrepancy.

3. **Person-setting variables.** Variables assumed to influence attention were placed in the following categories:
   a. **Visitor characteristics:** including sex, age, knowledge, attitudes, and "other individual differences." These characteristics all refer to the past history of the individual.
   b. **Exhibit characteristics:** Koran listed only four types of exhibits: static, dynamic, walk-through, and nonspecified. It is not clear how other characteristics such as size and organization of exhibit elements would be considered in his model.
   c. **Visitor processing activities:** attention, coding, strategies, rules, memory storage, retrieval, and other processing and orienting procedures. Koran and his colleagues examined processes such as Salomon's amount of invested energy expended (AIME) (Koran, Koran & Foster, 1988) and perspective taking (Ellis, 1993).
4. **Explanatory processes.** "Visitor processing activities" is one category in Koran's model. These activities included attention, coding, strategies, rules, memory storage, retrieval, and other processing and orienting procedures. These processes were not explained in enough detail to critique other than to note that they rely on psychological processes.
5. **Inferred outcomes.** Koran and Koran (1986a) included learning, knowledge [acquisition], curiosity, psychomotor development, interest, appreciation, and motivation" as "desired outcomes" from the museum experience.

Summary and Critique

Similar to Shettel's approach, Koran and his colleagues provided a model that included both "visitor" (person) and "setting" categories. Stopping and viewing time are two important measures of attention in his framework. His category of "exhibit characteristics" (i.e., static, dynamic, walk-through, nonspecified) was relatively nonspecific and did not identify the important design variables (size of objects, organization of exhibit elements) that others have recognized as important. His category of "desired outcome" includes the products of sustained engagement of attention (i.e., learning) as well as curiosity and motivation. He did not provide a detailed explanation of the mechanisms that tie together all of the concepts and variables he identified.

Gianna Moscardo and Ellen Langer

Gianna Moscardo is one of several researchers who have invoked Ellen Langer's (1989) concept of mindfulness-mindlessness to visitor attention. Langer describes "mindfulness" as " . . . a heightened state of involvement and wakefulness or being in the present." Langer explicitly argues that being mindful is always a good thing; being mindless is not. My understanding is that Langer's concept of mindfulness implies deeply engaged attention, but all deeply engaged attention is not being mindful. She also seems to imply that being in a broadly unfocused state of attention is not being mindful, although the way the concept is presented seems to leave a number of ambiguous questions.

Moscardo's (1999) approach to the "mindfulness" concept seems to differ from Langer's in at least three ways: (1) it is restricted to museum/tourism settings rather than applied to all mental activity; (2) it does not insist that being mindful is always possible, appropriate, or necessary; and (3) it places more emphasis on the importance of environmental influences. Because it is a restricted application of the concept of "mindfulness," it meets my definition of a "model" rather than a "theory" (see Chapter 1).

1. **Continuum.** Langer recognized only two distinct mental states: mindfulness or mindlessness. When one is mindful, one is open to learning, more likely to think creatively, and more deeply engaged with one's environment. Langer's two-state concept (mindfulness-mindlessness) is obviously not equivalent to the continuum of attention, although there seems to be some connection between mindfulness and engaged attention. Apparently, engaged attention is a necessary but not sufficient condition for mindfulness. Moscardo's writings do not seem to indicate one way or another how mindfulness relates to engaged attention.
2. **Response-impact measures.** If visitors are mindful, then they are more likely to recall exhibit content; they are also more likely to feel in control, to feel they are competent or have achieved something, and to feel more satisfied than if they are mindless. Response measures, therefore, might include self-report data of feeling in control, competent, and satisfied as well as knowledge acquisition data.
3. **Person-setting variables.** Moscardo argued that to encourage mindfulness, the setting should provide new and different surroundings, varied conditions, and individual control and choice. Her book outlined the conditions likely to create the atmosphere for mindful attention to occur.
4. **Explanatory mechanisms.** Mindfulness-mindlessness is the major construct identified. It is assumed to operate in a toggle-switch-like fashion. It is either on or off. The right conditions in the environment apparently stimulates mindful attention.
5. **Inferred outcomes.** Increased mindfulness apparently results in learning, satisfaction, and other desirable outcomes.

Summary and Critique

The mindfulness-mindlessness construct assumes a two-state process. When mindful, you are more likely to learn and process exhibit content in a meaningful way. When mindless, you are more likely to respond in a stereotyped manner, using old habits and schema, and fail to process information deeply. One difficulty with this approach is that it may not be falsifiable: there is no way to disprove it. The construct may be too vague to have good predictive validity.

Another difficulty is that logically, it seems counter to the fact that when we are searching an exhibit, we cannot be highly focused. If we were constantly in a mindful state, we would be too focused, filtering out important things in the environment. You might be in serious danger, for example, if you were mindfully reading a book as you crossed the street. To be aware of the dangers involved in crossing the street, your attention must be unfocused, being aware of traffic approaching in both directions, etc.

John Falk and Lynn Dierking

Falk and Dierking (1992, 2012) place considerable importance on the concept of "visitor agenda." Although not an explicit theory/model of visitor attention, it qualifies for this discussion since it attempts to predict what visitors will pay attention to and ultimately learn during their visit. The concept of "visitor agenda" is part of their "contextual model of learning" in which the interaction among personal, sociocultural, and physical contexts provides the basis of visitor experiences. In their 1992 book, Falk and Dierking suggested that knowledge, attitudes, experience, expectations, and visiting group characteristics "merge to create an agenda for the visitor." They recently updated this book and have added identity-related motivations to the "personal context":

> Collectively, a visitor's identity-related motivations, along with his expectations, prior interest, and knowledge, create an agenda for the visit. The visitor agendas more than anything else, including even the realities of the museum's exhibitions and/or programs, shape the museum experience (Falk & Dierking, 2012, p. 99).

Clearly, this quote indicates that the major responsibility of paying attention within museums is that of visitor agendas, or what visitors bring to the museum. The Falk-Dierking context model places only minor importance on setting factors such as exhibit design. The physical setting seems to serve as a passive place for the identity-related motivations to reveal themselves.

While Falk and Dierking suggest a benefit-cost decision-making mechanism for choosing to visit a museum, they did not extend this principle to the visitor experience once in the museum. They seem to imply that the benefits of satisfying an agenda will overcome the cost of time and effort required to engage with exhibits.

Identity (as an element of the visitor agenda) has been used to explain why people visit, what they see and do while visiting, and what learning occurs as a result of their experience. Several authors have questioned the Falk-Dierking model in terms of whether or not it is consistent with identity theory as well as the adequacy of empirical support for the model (Bickford, 2010; Rowe & Nickels, 2011; Dawson & Jensen, 2011). Since "identity" overlaps with other visitor agenda variables, I will leave to others further discussion of the merits of the identity model used by Falk and his followers. Instead, I will examine the concept of "agenda" (sans identity) and discuss how agendas might influence attention during a museum visit.

The following assumptions seem consistent with how the Falk-Dierking agenda concept relates to paying attention:

1. The agenda comprises a number of variables representing what visitors bring to their museum visit.
2. Agendas more than setting variables will predict visitor attention to exhibits and ultimately what is learned.
3. The pattern of attention to exhibit elements during a visit determines what is learned.

Several studies have examined the impact of visitor agendas (e.g., Briseño-Garzon, Anderson, & Anderson, 2007; Falk, Moussouri, & Coulson, 1998; Moussouri, 1999). For example, Falk et al. (1998) studied the impact of visitor agendas at the National Museum of Natural History in Washington, D.C. They found that two categories, education and entertainment, were significantly correlated with learning (as measured by their Personal Meaning Map [PMM] measure of learning). Most of the participants gave multiple reasons for their visit, but they did not report details of this data. As a second element of visitor agenda, "strategy" was divided into three categories: unfocused, moderately focused, and focused. This perspective of "focusing" as a general strategy seems to imply that visitors are consistent throughout their visit in their degree of focus and consequently would differ in terms of their level of engagement with exhibits. Unfortunately, the focus data were not reported.

If previsit agendas are the most powerful predictors of what visitors will see and do during their visit, then the actual museum experience should have minimal impact on these agendas. However, Briseño-Garzon, Anderson, and Anderson (2007) found that visitor agendas were modified as the visit progressed due to such experiences as development of a particular interest, fascination, or concern during the visit; children's attention span, restlessness, and endurance; show times; crowdedness; and weather conditions. " . . . [T]he study shows that agendas and agenda consolidation were a continuing dynamic, and non-linear process where multiple events converged and influenced one another."

Given the Briseño-Garzon et al. study, it may be important to distinguish between "agenda" in general and "previsit agenda." Clearly, agendas continually change during the visit. To claim that the previsit agenda is the most important factor in shaping the museum experience may be premature. Additional research is needed to sort out the relative contributions of what visitors bring to the visit from the impact of the visit.

1. **Attention continuum.** The visitor agenda approach does not specifically address the notion of stages of attention, although the "degree of focus" measure seems to imply that an unfocused visitor will deeply engage with very little exhibit content during a visit. An agenda might dictate how often a visitor stops to view (capture), whether one's attention becomes focused, and whether and how often the visitor would read text labels and how often one might be involved in other deeply engaged activities.
2. **Response-impact measures.** Falk and Dierking proposed a unique way to measure visitor attention. The PMM is a method of measuring learning involving a detailed interview that attempts to reveal an individual's learning in four general areas. Since it relies on recall of content rather than recognition, it would be less sensitive than a methodology using recognition to what visitors actually learn. A more detailed discussion of PMM can be found in Chapter 4.
3. **Person-setting factors.** The context model suggests that personal factors (e.g., education, motivation for attending, identity, interest, and similar variables) have the major influence on attention within the exhibitions. Physical context (e.g., exhibit design variables) appears to be limited to providing a stage for agendas to reveal themselves.
4. **Explanatory mechanisms.** According to Falk and Dierking, "agenda" is the strongest influence on visitor attention during their visit. Falk and Dierking did not address the findings reported by Briseño-Garzon, et al. that demonstrate how family agendas change during the course of the visit.
5. **Inferred outcomes.** Visitor agendas might be assumed to influence the range of inferred outcomes. However, learning and effect are the only outcomes that have been examined so far in studies.

Summary and Critique

While the notion of visitor agenda is an appealing concept with obvious potential for a better understanding of visitor attention, there is a need to define the concept more precisely and flesh out the various variables and processes that might be involved. As it stands, the "agenda" construct needs additional detail to be a powerful predictor of attention. An agenda is a plan. If the definition of visitor agenda is restricted to previsit plans, some of the confusion and ambiguity associated with changes during the visit may be reduced. Since no one has examined the impact of agenda on visitor attention directly, it remains to be demonstrated how much previsit agendas influence visitor attention relative to other factors such as exhibit design. Since previsit agendas are significantly altered during the course of a visit, a more detailed notion of agenda is needed to determine what aspects of the agenda might stay constant and what aspects might change.

The studies that have examined visitor agendas (and/or identity-related motivations) have not examined how agendas and/or identities influence attention at specific exhibits. These studies have used a combination of self-report and knowledge acquisition measures. When visitors demonstrate learning, there is no direct evidence of how engaged attention during their exhibit viewing contributed to that learning.

Jay Rounds

Rounds (2004) applied optimal foraging theory to visitor attention. In general, optimal foraging theory suggests that the "value" of a choice is determined by a ratio of benefit divided by search and handling time (cost). This theory has been applied to predator-prey behavior in which the predator must choose among available prey, taking into account the benefit (e.g., energy obtained from consuming the prey) and the time necessary to search for and handle the prey once it is caught. It has also been applied to animals and human gatherers searching for edible plants. More recently, it has been applied to information foraging (Pirolli & Card, 1999) typical on Internet searches.

Rounds suggests a rule-governed version of foraging in museum exhibitions. Three sets of rules are assumed to guide visitor behavior: search rules, attention rules, and quitting rules.

1. **Continuum.** Rounds' three sets of rules appear to recognize that attention occurs in a sequence of stages from capture (search rules) to focus (attention rules) to engagement (quit rules).

2. **Response-impact measures.** Rounds did not specifically suggest measures of attention, although stopping and viewing time were implied by his discussion.

3. **Person-setting variables.** In addition to what the visitor brings to the museum, the content of the exhibition influences the level of curiosity and interest visitors might have in exhibit elements. Decision-making processes (ratio of benefit divided by search and handle time) also play a large role in Rounds' viewpoint.

4. **Explanatory mechanisms.** Psychological processes of curiosity and decision-making take a leading role in Rounds' model. Curiosity is the motivation for attending to exhibits and the value ratio (perceived satisfaction of curiosity divided by cost in terms of perceived time and effort of commitment to attend). Decision rules are divided into three areas: search, attention, and quitting.

   a. **Search rules** (guidelines for scanning exhibit elements):

      1. *"Assume that the interest landscape is rugged."* "The visitor's initial search strategy should be based on scanning widely throughout the museum, rather than focusing the search only in one area" (Rounds, 2004; p. 402).

      2. *"Get moving."* Don't use up valuable time planning; start with the nearest exhibit that has potential and get on with the search for content that satisfies curiosity.

      3. *"Scan exhibits."* Don't make a commitment to each exhibit element; maximize the chance of finding as many potentially interesting elements as possible.

      4. *"Follow the crowd to water, but be slow to drink."* Look for exhibit elements where other visitors appear to be engaged, but apply the attention rules before engaging.

   b. **Attention rules** (rules that indicate when to stop searching):

      1. *"Follow your nose."* Foraging theory has introduced the concept of "scent." Text panels with too many words, difficult jargon, etc. give a negative scent and should be avoided.

      2. *"Don't make large down payments."* Don't invest a large amount of time trying to understand what the exhibit is all about. If you can't figure it out quickly, move on to something with more potential.

      3. *"Satisfice."* Rounds adopts Simon's concept (1956), which suggests that decision-making cannot be perfect. Stop searching when you find something that meets your basic criterion rather than looking for something that is perfect. "Satisfice" suggests a satisfactory target rather than the best target.

c. **Quitting rules** (rules that specify when to stop attending to an exhibit element):

1. *"Cut your losses."* Give up on an exhibit element that does not show immediate promise.
2. *"Three strikes, you're out."* Quit the exhibition hall or gallery if you encounter several exhibits in a row that do not satisfy curiosity.
3. *"Stop eating when your appetite is satisfied."* When interest from a particular exhibit element is satisfied, move on.
4. *"Don't stay for leftovers."* ". . . quit when new selections prove to have less interest value than the average value you have received for elements up to that point" (Rounds, 2004, p. 406).

5. **Inferred outcomes.** The satisfaction of curiosity appears to be the major outcome of interest in Round's model.

Summary and Critique

Rounds' approach is both contemporary and unique compared with other approaches. Optimal foraging has become a significant theory in biology, psychology, and information science and has intriguing potential relevance to museum visitors. It is the first approach to visitor attention that is based on a decision-making model, one that is similar to other benefit/cost economic approaches to choice.

The major weakness of his model may be the difficulty required to test the validity of the search, attention, and quitting rules. At first glance, one might think that simple self-report data would allow us to assess when his decision rules (search, attention, and quitting) are being applied. However, he has noted that the decision-making process involved is not necessarily a conscious process. Obviously, animal predators are unlikely to apply conscious reason to their predatory efforts, yet the model applies well to animals. Since Rounds offered no data to support his model, only time will tell how useful it will be to museum professionals.

Other Viewpoints

I am aware of three Ph.D. dissertations that are relevant to visitor attention (Carlson, 1993; Ellis, 1993; Lightner, 1998). In addition, Beverly Serrell's work provides an additional example of how visitor studies' professionals have dealt with visitor attention.

Carlson (1993) invoked a combination of traditional cognitive processing approaches with Langer's mindfulness-mindlessness construct. While he provided an excellent review of some of the literature, his model appears to imply that physical activity is a necessary element of mindful attention. As with Rounds, he provided a model of visitor attention, but did not provide any data.

Ellis (1993) examined two viewing strategies: (1) viewing an exhibit in a prescribed order and (2) taking different cognitive perspectives while viewing. The study showed that both techniques were successful in influencing visitor attention and learning. Ellis did not propose a model or theory of attention, but the study does show that managing the sequence of visitor attention and the mindset or perspective can influence how much and what visitors might pay attention to and learn.

Lightner (1993) proposed a four-factor model of attention. Interest and relevance of the exhibit were personal factors that interact with exhibit design; the result is the impact on attention. One of his major points is that there are two kinds of interest: enduring personal interest—a stable quality of the individual; and curiosity—a more general, common attribute of the population. Relevance provides the motivation that the situation has personal importance. However, Lightner's model does not attempt to identify the exhibit characteristics that influence visitor attention. Interest and relevance as motivators may be insufficient.

Beverly Serrell (1998) published a monograph in which she summarized attention data from 110 exhibition evaluations conducted by a number of professionals in a variety of museum settings. She proposed two new measures of attention (exhibit success): sweep-rate index (SRI) is defined as the average total time visitors spend in the exhibition divided by the square footage. This measure allows one to compare exhibitions of different sizes in terms of how quickly visitors move through exhibit spaces. The other measure, diligent visitors (%DV), is calculated by comparing the percentage of visitors who stopped at more than half of the exhibit elements. This measure suggests how thoroughly visitors use the entire exhibition. Serrell's model offers a simple method to assess exhibition effectiveness: higher levels of attention are associated with moving slowly through the exhibition and stopping at more than one-half of the exhibit elements. Similar to the Lakota model, this approach is not diagnostic since it does not identify characteristics of exhibit elements that make it successful. The approach does not propose any explanatory mechanisms for connecting the response measures of attention (e.g., moving slowly, stopping at a large number of exhibit elements) and the variables that might influence attention. The most appropriate use of this approach may be for summative evaluation, in which no additional changes are planned to the exhibition.

Summary of Theoretical Models

The theories and models described in this chapter give credence to both the importance and the complexity of visitor attention. Each approach offers at least a partial insight into our understanding of visitor attention. Robinson and Melton provided the groundwork for later research in visitor attention. Shettel, Lakota, and Koran were the first to attempt a theoretical framework for visitor attention. Screven attempted to apply relevant research literature from psychology and education to visitor attention. Moscardo introduced Langer's mindfulness-mindlessness construct to attention. Falk and Dierking emphasized the importance of visitor agendas on the visitor experience. Rounds applied optimal foraging theory, one of several approaches based on a benefit/cost ratio. While the review of theories/models is not exhaustive, it hopefully represents the diversity of ideas and approaches that can be applied to visitor attention.

My attention-value model described in Chapter 5 attempts to incorporate and expand upon many of the ideas of the theories/models discussion in this chapter. The theoretical viewpoints of people in this chapter have provided the foundation for the approach taken in this book.

NOTE

1. Self-report measures were not used by Robinson and Melton, presumably because they were viewed with suspicion by much of mainstream, behavioral psychologists of that time.

chapter 4

Inferred Outcomes of Engaged Attention

▹ **KEY IDEAS** ◃

- Once attention is engaged, many desirable outcomes can be inferred.
- Inferred outcomes include learning, immersion, flow, and attention restoration.
- The large number of outcomes inferred from engaged attention in museums suggests both the creativity of those proposing the outcomes and the breadth and depth of the museum experience.

Introduction

The visitor literature contains numerous examples of studying the inferred outcomes of engaged attention. These outcomes are logically deduced from the relationship between person-setting variables and measures of engaged attention (see Table 1.1 in Chapter 1 for an explanation of the model). It is important to realize that we do not observe outcomes such as learning directly, but must infer them from a test of knowledge or performance of some behavior. The purpose of this chapter is to illustrate the variety of ways engaged attention can be tied to inferred outcomes.

Some of the examples in this chapter emphasize the methods of measuring engaged attention (e.g., informal learning, inquiry learning, family learning, Personal Meaning Mapping), whereas others emphasize design principles that create engaged attention (e.g., exhibit efficiency, Russell's design list). Still others propose a psychological construct that emerges when attention is engaged (e.g., flow, immersion, restoration). All of these inferred outcomes invoke engaged attention of some sort as evidence. While the examples of inferred outcomes in this chapter are not exhaustive, they do demonstrate the rich variety of outcomes that are assumed to result from engaging attention to

Attention and Value: Keys to Understanding Museum Visitors by Stephen Bitgood, 54–63.

museum media. This variety provides additional support for the importance of studying attention.

Informal Learning (Free-Choice Learning)

Learning is usually the most important goal of exhibition centers that profess to educate the public as part of their mission. Despite general agreement that learning should be a goal, there is little agreement about what museum learning really is, what it should be, or even how to measure it.

Among its other names, learning has been called "informal learning" and "free-choice learning" to distinguish it from classroom learning (e.g., Falk & Dierking, 2000). However it is defined, there is agreement that not only does it differ from classroom learning, but also that visitors really do learn something (e.g., Bitgood, 2011b, pp. 90–109; Falk & Dierking, 2000; Hein, 1998).

Museum learning may be difficult to study for several reasons:

1. Museum learning is not directly observed; it must be inferred from some measures of visitor attention (visitor verbal and/or written statements about exhibit content). Learning has been defined and measured in many different ways by researchers and evaluators. The approaches described in this chapter give some idea of the wide variations in how museum learning is approached. While classroom learning emphasizes abstract semantic knowledge, museum learning is generally more broadly defined.
2. There is considerable pressure from funding agencies to demonstrate that learning really occurs in museums, but museum professionals generally reject the narrow learning criteria of formal education.
3. The relationship between formal and informal learning is not always clear since there is considerable overlap in terms of both knowledge domain and media. Museum field trips are often part of academic experience for children, and the impact of these experiences is often closely related to classroom experiences. Museum programs frequently include lectures for the general public (as well as school groups) that are often similar in form to classroom lectures.
4. Many have argued that the most important impact of the museum experience is to stimulate further learning at some later time. According to this argument, long-term impact of museum learning must be assessed. However, long-term impact assessment is difficult to assess because of all the confounding variables that are present after the individual has left the museum.

Inquiry Learning

Sue Allen and Joshua Gutwill (2009) reported a project at the Exploratorium in which visitors were trained to engage in inquiry behaviors. Inquiry behaviors were defined as a series of steps (observing, asking questions, testing hypotheses, etc.). The study found that training visitor groups to ask a question to drive investigation and to interpret the results of their investigation at the end improved the chances of inquiry behavior at a subsequent exhibit, and was rated as enjoyable by participants. Since "inquiry" is usually considered an important aspect of scientific thinking, the demonstration that museums can stimulate this type of behavior is important.

Family Learning (PISEC Project)

Minda Borun's work on family learning with the Philadelphia collaborative (PISEC) project (Borun, Chambers, & Cleghorn, 1996; Borun, Chambers, Dritsas, & Johnson, 1997; Borun & Dritsas, 1997) provides a methodology to measure different levels of engaged attention related to informal learning. She and her colleagues suggest three levels of learning: (1) *identifying* (describing simple activity, naming or group animals); (2) *describing* (describing specific animal or plant species, making a general connection to other situations); and (3) *interpreting* and *applying* (describing how different species support compete or adapt, mentions system of classification). These three levels of learning suggest different degrees of attention engagement. *Interpreting* requires a deeper level of engaged attention than *describing* or *identifying*. The PISEC method of measuring family learning is not only diagnostic (the impact of each exhibit display can be assessed), but indicates that learning occurs on multiple levels.

Knowledge Hierarchy Assessment

Deborah Perry[1] (1993, 2012) has proposed a knowledge hierarchy assessment technique "based on a careful examination of the exhibition, discussions with exhibit developers, and in-depth interviews with visitors."

> The knowledge hierarchy . . . is based on the assumption that inherent in each exhibit is an internal knowledge structure . . . . A knowledge hierarchy is simply a description of [the] range of . . . knowledge visitors have about a topic, but within the context of the exhibit (Perry, 2012, p. 45).

Perry's approach assumes that: (1) there is a knowledge structure to an exhibition; (2) the structure communicates this to visitors; and (3) this knowledge can be measured. The technique is individualized for each exhibition. Hierarchies are usually divided into five or six levels ranging from "I don't know" to "sophisticated understanding of the exhibit concept."

Personal Meaning Mapping (PMM)

Using a constructivist rationale, John Falk has suggested Personal Meaning Mapping (PMM) as a method for assessing learning in exhibit environments (e.g., Adelman, Falk, & James, 2000; Falk, Moussouri, & Coulson, 1998). Participants are asked to write words, ideas, images, phrases, or thoughts that come to mind related to exhibit content. These words form the basis of an open-ended interview in which visitors are encouraged to explain why they wrote what they did and to expand on their thoughts and ideas. Responses are recorded on the same paper, and different colors of ink are used for prompted versus unprompted responses. PMMs from previsit are compared with postvisit PMMs. Changes in the following dimensions are examined: (1) *quantity of appropriate vocabulary* (counting number of relevant words/phrases written down by visitor); (2) *breadth of a visitor's understanding* (range of conceptual understanding measured as the change in the quantity of appropriate concepts used); (3) *depth of visitors' understanding* (how detailed and complex descriptions were within a conceptual category [e.g., how many different types of gems did visitors list?]); and (4) according to Falk, Moussouri, & Coulson (1998), the fourth criterion is *mastery* (the overall facility with which visitors described their understanding, rated on a 1 to 4 scale, novice to expert). However, Adelman, Falk, and James (2000) listed the fourth criterion as "*emotional intensity*."

It is not clear how PMM differs from other approaches in terms of assessing visitors' knowledge acquired within an exhibition. One of the methodological difficulties with this technique is testing the same individuals before and after their visit. Adelman, Falk, and James (2000) compared the results of a pre- and posttested group with a posttest-only group and claimed to find no significant differences. There are at least three reasons why no difference was found between the posttest-only and the pre- and posttest groups:

1. PMM may not have the usual methodological bias of pretesting individuals. A pretesting interview would usually sensitize visitors to exhibit content, making them more aware of possible issues and subject matter they will encounter and resulting in closer attention to exhibit material relevant to the previsit discussion.
2. PMM may not be sensitive enough to detect a difference because it relies on recall rather than recognition. Since recognition is a more sensitive measure, recall measures as used in the PMM method tend to underestimate the depth of knowledge.

3. The method may be prone to subjective analysis. The relatively unstructured method of analysis used in PMM may encourage finding (or not finding) what the researcher wants to find.

Additional research by independent researchers may clarify this issue. Comparisons of PMM with traditional measures of learning might be helpful, as would independent reliability assessments of scoring. The cost-effectiveness of the method may also be an issue.

Exhibit Efficiency

Screven's (1992) article on motivating visitors to read labels reviewed many factors that are involved in motivating visitors to attend to exhibit labels. Later, Screven (1999) updated his position on visitor attention and learning. Here, we will focus on only one of his concepts: "exhibit efficiency" or "the time and effort it takes to process a display's content." Efficiency is hypothesized to be a function of both personal factors (e.g., time limitations, fatigue, individual attitudes, viewer's interest in learning), and the design characteristics of the exhibit. Exhibit efficiency is related to the notion of value ratio in that it includes both benefits and costs of engaging attention on exhibit elements. Unfortunately, Screven did not specify a workable methodology for assessing and predicting exhibit efficiency.

Russell's Design List

Bob Russell (2000) provides a provocative list of ten suggestions for designing engaging exhibits:

1. provide advance organizers
2. design accessible, attractive, inviting, involving environments
3. design accessible and easy-to-use exhibits
4. present real objects/phenomena
5. meet visitor expectations
6. provide entry points to meet individual visitors' needs
7. offer visitors choices, control, feedback, and success
8. support direct experiences with labels, staff explainers, and opportunities for cooperative engagement
9. provide support for follow-up educational experiences
10. evaluate

I suspect that not many museum professionals would disagree with the ten suggestions. But are they sufficient to guide exhibit designers? Minimal detail accompanies these suggestions. For example, under his first point (provide advance organizers), he suggests that designers "provide visitors with obvious starting points." This advice is important but open to interpretation. Does this mean provide the usual contents of conceptual orientation: what there is to see and do, how the exhibition is organized, and the key ideas of the exhibition? In his second point (design accessible, attractive, inviting, involving environments) he suggests "design for non-intimidating environments and non-distracting environments." What is an "intimidating" environment? Do visitors really get intimidated? Can we identify factors that are intimidating to visitors and ensure that we eliminate them? What is a "distracting" environment? In an open environment such as most science centers, movement and noises from other exhibits are distracting. Should the science center concept be redefined to eliminate such distractions?

Another difficulty is that the design principles are not organized into an integrated theory or model of visitor attention. If the list of these ten points were incorporated into a conceptual system, they might be more useful to practitioners and to researchers who wish to tease out implications of the theory.

Other Types of Inferred Outcomes

In addition to the outcomes described here that are all associated with learning, a number of other types of inferred outcomes are commonly described in the visitor literature.

Simulated Immersion

Some experiences in museums and theme parks are designed to deeply engage visitors by providing a feeling of being immersed in a particular time and place. Such an experience is assumed to create both a deeper engagement of attention and greater satisfaction.

Years ago I suggested that Jon Coe's (1986) concept of landscape immersion be expanded into a more general notion of "simulated immersion" (Bitgood, 1990, 1991, 2011b). Immersion is defined as the illusion of "feeling in a specific time and place." Coe, a zoo designer, is part of a movement of landscape immersion that has come to dominate zoo design. "The visitor leaves the familiar grounds of an urban park called a zoological garden, and actually enters into the simulated habitat of the animals" (Coe, 1986, p. 9). A similar movement of immersion can be found in living history museums (e.g., Yellis, 1990). A section of my 2011 book *Social Design in Museums: The Psychology of Visitor Studies* (Bitgood, 2011a; pp. 102–198) discusses immersion and includes descriptions of empirical studies that may help to better understand the phenomenon. Chapter 39 ("Immersion Experiences in Museums") provides an update in my thinking of immersion. For additional references on immersion, see Gyllenhaal (2002).

The literature (see Bitgood, 2011b) suggests that at least some of the following person-setting factors are involved in immersion experiences: realism of the illusionary experiences, dimensionality (three-dimensional environment), multisensory stimulation, making the subject come to life, use of mental imagery, and a lack of interfering distractions from feeling in the time and place. Measures of immersion usually include rating scales of the defining criteria (e.g., degree to which the visitor feels in the time and place).

In several of my studies, I used postvisit ratings of the immersion qualities of natural history museum exhibits at the Anniston Museum of Natural History (e.g., Bitgood, 1990). Ratings of impact to such experiences as "feeling in the time and place" and "natural" were consistent with the exhibit characteristics such as being surrounded by the exhibit space (walk-through diorama). Harvey, Loomis, Bell, and Marino (1998) found similar results at the Denver Museum of Nature and Science: visitors' feelings of immersion were correlated with interactive components, multisensory stimulation, and dynamic displays.

Flow

Csikszentmihalyi (1990) has adapted and further developed Maslow's concept of "peak experience" in his construct of "flow." Flow is assumed to involve completely focused motivation during some activity, making it an example of deeply engaged attention. Flow is accompanied by energized focus, full involvement, and a feeling of accomplishment or success in performance.

Harvey, Loomis, Bell, and Marino (1998) examined the impact of renovated exhibits at the Denver Museum of Nature and Science in terms of flow. They reported that design characteristics such as interactive components, multisensory stimulation, and dynamic display contribute to visitor ratings of flow.

Attention Restoration

Kaplan developed the theory of attention restoration (e.g., Kaplan, 1983; Kaplan, Bardwell, & Slakter, 1993; Kaplan & Kaplan, 1989). The stresses of everyday life are assumed to decrease the capacity to manage one's own attention. This condition creates "directed attention fatigue" (Kaplan & Kaplan, 1989; Kaplan, Bardwell, & Slakter, 1993). Directed attention fatigue makes it difficult to concentrate and relax. Kaplan argued that people search out experiences to reduce this fatigue.

According to this theory, restoration of directed fatigue requires four components: being away, extent, fascination, and compatibility.

1. **Being away.** Being away from the stress of everyday life is divided into two elements: physical and mental. One can become geographically removed from the stressful environment or change one's psychological frame of reference to a relaxing activity. Both approaches are possible ways to accomplish "being away."
2. **Extent.** A setting with "extent" creates "a whole other world" if it is rich and coherent enough. Examples include natural environments that give a sense of being in another world.
3. **Fascination.** Fascination implies something of high interest. However, "hard fascination" may not contribute to restoration, while "soft fascination" does. Hard fascinating events such as violence may grab attention, but not lead to restoration. Soft fascination such as watching a sunset, on the other hand, is more likely to facilitate restoration.
4. **Compatibility.** The environment must be supportive of the individual's goals or purpose for being in the setting. If a visitor arrives at a botanic garden with the purpose of enjoying the beauty and relaxing, then the setting is compatible.

Kaplan, Bardwell, and Slakter (1993) examined the restorative impact of a museum visit. They first performed a content analysis of focus group responses to art museums that was part of a Getty Foundations study. They found that categories of responses were consistent with restoration theory. Next, visitors completed postvisit surveys on the restorative aspects of their visit. The results suggest that not everyone has a restorative museum experience; visitors who feel most comfortable with the museum environment are more likely to experience restoration.

The relationship between restoration and visitor attention needs further study. When museum visitors have restorative experiences, to what and at what level are they engaged? Is deep engagement of attention necessary to create restoration? Are repeat visitors more likely to experience restoration?

Empathic Dramatic Engagement

Du Toit and Dye (2008) describe another approach to inferred outcomes; they call it "empathic dramatic engagement" in art museums. Visitors construct meaning by ". . . actively [reaching] out to new knowledge contained within the exhibition and its narratives, and contextualiz[ing] significant affective and cognitive percepts through a process of appropriation, assimilation, accommodation, and identification" (pp. 73–74). According to the authors, this process is the product of (1) experience (both previous and in-museum experience), (2) narrative (visitor constructs a "story" related to exhibit content), and (3) play (imaginative association and elaboration of ideas). Measurement of empathic dramatic engagement is carried out by analysis of postvisit audio recordings of informal conversations (narratives) be-tween the evaluators and the visitors. The discussions are examined in terms of character, plot, dialog, setting, and suspension of disbelief. Character "refers to the essential nature of a work of art." Plot refers to the narratives that visitors construct using their memories and imaginations to "fill in the gaps" between what information is given and what makes sense as part of the story. Dialog "is often the medium through which the plot progresses. . . . [It is] manifest in both explicit language and implicit non-discursive communication" (p. 80). Setting "provides a staged world within which the characters operate" (p. 81). Suspension of disbelief and imaginative elaboration is "the willingness of a person to accept as true the premises of a work of fiction . . . and a willingness . . . to overlook limitations or shortcomings of the medium" (p. 81). Incidence of the above dramatic elements reported from this study were as follows: 100 percent of visitors included dialog; 90 percent included suspension of disbelief; 60 percent, character; 55 percent, plot; and 25 percent, setting.

Experience-Benefit Analysis

As previously noted, engaged attention can result in more than learning outcomes. Jan Packer (2008) examined the experiences (satisfying and restorative) and perceived benefits (psychological well-being, subjective well-being, and restoration) of a museum visit. Visitors were interviewed following their visit. Satisfying experiences were mentioned in 93 percent of interviews, including experiences associated with objects, cognition, introspection, and social interaction. Restorative elements were mentioned in 73 percent of interviews. For benefits and outcomes, psychological well-being was mentioned in 59 percent, subjective well-being in 11 percent, and restoration in 57 percent of interviews.

Conclusions

This chapter has briefly described a number of inferred outcomes associated with engaged attention. The variety of outcomes listed in this chapter give testimony both to the richness of deeply engaged attention and to the imaginations of those who have proposed these outcomes.

Some of the inferred outcomes involve learning: informal or "free-choice" learning, family learning, inquiry learning, knowledge hierarchy assessment, and PMM. Each of these outcomes reflects the thinking of those proposing this type of outcome.

Other inferred outcomes in this chapter refer to a more holistic, complex experience than may be involved with learning: simulated immersion, flow, attention restoration, and empathetic dramatic engagement. These outcomes place more emphasis on affective components of the experience than is generally implied with cognitive learning outcomes. Of course, affective and cognitive impacts are not mutually exclusive, and all theories and models of inferred outcomes believe that the museum experience can deliver a combination of the two.

The possible outcomes of engaged attention are many. Given the number of possible alternative inferred outcomes, we have at least three alternatives. We can celebrate the richness of the different possible types of museum experiences. Instead, we might conclude that the experience is impossible to study because of its complexity. Or, we can examine all of these possible outcomes more carefully to assess how they contribute to the visitor experience. My preference is to celebrate the diversity.

NOTE

1. Deborah Perry (2012) has more recently provided a detailed model of museum learning, which she calls "The Selinda Model of Visitor Learning." Since it has only recently been published, time did not allow inclusion of this model in this book.

chapter 5

Overview of The Attention-Value Model

▷ **KEY IDEAS** ◁

- The attention-value model argues that attention and value are key concepts in understanding museum visitors.
- Attention is viewed as a three-stage continuum: capture, focus, and engagement. Each stage is composed a unique set of response-impact measures (approach, stop, view, discuss content, etc.) and a unique combination of person-setting variables (agendas, personal interest, exhibit design, etc.) that influence visitor responses.
- An economic definition of value (utility/cost) is applied to visitors. Value is a key motivational factor in determining to what visitors pay attention.
- The value ratio (utility or benefit/cost) examines visitor choice in terms of (1) utility/benefit (visitor variables such as interests and preferences) and (2) cost (time and effort or workload).
- The available-alternative theorem, one of the implications of the value ratio, assumes the value of choosing to pay attention to a particular exhibit element is not fixed; it depends upon what alternatives are available at any moment.
- The small-cost theorem argues that since people are more sensitive to cost (time, effort) than utility, the cost of paying attention should be as small as possible. For example, keep time and effort of reading text labels at a minimum.
- Other important variables that influence attention include physiological and mental states (e.g., fatigue, satiation), decision-making processes, and learned strategies and behavior patterns.

Introduction

The ultimate goals of museum exhibitions generally include the following outcomes: (1) to provide meaningful learning experiences, (2) to change

Attention and Value: Keys to Understanding Museum Visitors by Stephen Bitgood, 64–73.

attitudes, (3) to create intellectual and emotional experiences that stimulate curiosity and excitement, and/or (4) to facilitate some of the other outcomes (e.g., immersion, flow, renewal) described in the previous chapter. However, these goals cannot be achieved without understanding and managing the processes of attention. Unlike the paradox of which comes first, the chicken or the egg, there is no doubt that *attention must occur before learning.* While much of the informal educational literature has focused on outcomes such as learning, often neglected are the processes of attention that are responsible for learning outcomes. Learning may flow easily once attention is deeply engaged. But how can we structure the exhibition experience so that we obtain deeply engaged attention? When deeply engaged attention does happen, are visitors more likely to persist at constructing meaning from exhibit content? Once these questions are answered, we can ask what else is necessary to obtain the desired learning outcome. No matter what theoretical viewpoint is applied to museum learning, deeply engaged attention is required.

In the first chapter, I define attention and discuss its complexities. At first, these processes of attention may seem overwhelming and complicated. We can minimize some of the confusion by making clear the differences between attention and other concepts such as interest and learning by providing a conceptual framework based on research findings of how attention is related to other concepts, and by developing a theory or model that can guide us to design better visitor experiences. This chapter attempts to describe a model of attention that addresses these points.

The Attention-Value Model

The attention-value model incorporates findings from both visitor research collected in the last 80-plus years as well as from important elements of the theories/models of attention reviewed in the previous chapter.

The Model in a Nutshell

The attention-value model can be summarized in a simple formula:

ATTENTION = DETECTION + VALUE

This formula should be read as follows: the chances of paying attention to an exhibit element are directly related to (1) the ease of detecting the stimulus (e.g., exhibit object) and (2) the relative value associated with the experience of engaging attention to a specific exhibit element compared with alternative choices. The weighting of detection and value varies with the stage of attention. Detection is most important in the capture stage, and value has the highest weighting in the engagement stage. To understand how detection and value influence visitor attention, it is necessary to understand the psychological processes that involve what the visitor brings to the museum (person or visitor variables) and what is encountered in the museum setting (exhibit design, social influence, and other setting variables).

Briefly, the attention-value model can be summarized as follows:

1. **The continuum of attention.** Attention is conceived as a three-level continuum (capture, focus, engagement) in which attention varies from unfocused, shallow processing of information to highly focused, deep processing. If learning is to happen, then attention must be focused and deep processing of the exhibit content must occur.
2. **Uniqueness of each stage.** Each stage of attention contains a unique set of response indicators and a unique set of factors that influence attention at that stage. For example, in the capture stage, the detection of exhibit elements is of vital importance. In the focus stage, setting characteristics such as distractions and interest level determine whether visitors spend only a few seconds viewing or decide to move to the engagement stage, in which the value ratio associated with the exhibit element becomes most important.
3. **Detection and value.** The capture, focus, and engagement of vistor attention depend upon two major factors: detection and value. An exhibit object must first be detected by the visitor and then be perceived as having a sufficient level of value for visitors to invest the time and effort required for engaged attention.
4. **Detection refers to the ease with which an object/stimulus is noticed.** Some stimuli (e.g., loud noise) demand attention. Other stimuli (objects that do not fall within the visitor's line of sight) may remain completely undetected. The capture of attention relies heavily on the processes of detection, which depends upon sensory-perceptual processes.
5. **Visual search processes are closely related to detection.** Once attention is captured, what processes explain how visitors focus their attention? How visitors sequence their attention from one object or element to another is a critical aspect of what and how visitors pay attention.
6. **The value ratio is the primary motivator of paying attention.** The primary motivation for paying attention is perceived or actual value (a ratio of benefits or utility or satisfaction divided by costs such as time and effort) of the exhibit element. While benefits such as satisfying curiosity, enjoyment, and fun are an important part of what motivates attention, these benefits are offset by the costs in terms of time, effort, and money.

Psychological Processes in Visitor Attention

Detection and value are both complex concepts involving a number of psychological processes and variables.

Detection

The following briefly describes the sensory-perceptual processes that determine the ease with which a stimulus/object can be detected.

1. **Orienting reflex.** One of the basic survival reflexes in humans and animals is that of the orienting reflex. A powerful stimulus (loud noise, sudden movement, flash of light) automatically captures attention.
2. **Salience of stimuli.** By their nature, some stimuli have greater power to attract attention. Large size, good contrast from the background, and movement are some of the major characteristics that make an exhibit element salient.
3. **Sight lines.** Objects that fall easily within our line of sight have a greater chance of being detected and therefore capturing attention.
4. **Proximity of exhibit object to the visitor.** The shorter the distance between the visitor and an object, the more likely it will capture attention. In addition, an interpretive panel will be given more attention the closer it is to the object it interprets.
5. **Distraction.** Distraction occurs when attention is involuntarily shifted from one object to another or when the presence of multiple objects reduces attention to an object that is the focus of attention. One type of distraction (discussed above) is the orienting response to a loud noise, sudden movement, or flash of light that distracts attention away from an exhibit object to something else. When the orienting reflex shifts attention away from rather than toward a target exhibit element, it becomes a distraction. In addition, the presentation of multiple objects within a dense space may also create some perceptual distraction.

Visual Search

The goal-driven act of visually searching exhibits has not received adequate attention from visitor researchers and evaluators. The sequence of shifting attention from one object to another is of critical concern to how visitors distribute their attention within museums. Search patterns are closely related to detection processes because the pattern of sequential search determines what is detected. The complexity of these visual search problems is well documented in cognitive psychology (e.g., Corbetta & Shulman, 2002; Posner & Cohen, 1984).

1. **Serial (sequential) versus parallel (simultaneous) search.** A visitor may pay attention to one exhibit element after another in some type of logical order (serial or sequential search), or look at the whole complex of an exhibit and wait for something salient to "pop out" of the complex (parallel or simultaneous search). The search pattern is likely to be determined by the layout or organization of the exhibit elements. If there is a clear sequence or order from one element to another, sequential search is likely to occur. If the search pattern is not obvious, a simultaneous search is likely to occur. If the search is sequential, then each exhibit element is likely to have a chance to capture attention; but, if a simultaneous search occurs, attention to exhibit elements is likely to be irregular and spotty, with attention focused on only one or two elements.
2. **Within-exhibit search pattern.** The type of exhibit element influences search patterns (i.e., 3-D objects capture attention first, then photos and illustrations, and finally blocks of interpretive text) and learned habits or patterns of responding such as reading.
3. **Between-exhibits search pattern.** Switching attention from one exhibit display to another may depend upon a number of factors, including the perceived value of the alternatives available ("Why waste my time on this one when there is a more attractive one next to it?"). The physical relationship or distance between exhibit displays may also play a role—the closer they are together, the more likely there is to be a shift in attention. Sight lines from the approach location, etc., are also important.

A pathway through an exhibition that contains exhibits on both sides creates additional problems in managing attention. Especially in crowded conditions, visitors often do not move from one side to the other of a wide pathway (e.g., Bitgood, 2006). One-sided viewing is a common pattern, perhaps because it conserves steps and is a way to avoid encountering oncoming crowds.

The intended sequence, both within an exhibit display and between exhibits, should be made explicit; otherwise, there is a strong possibility of visitors misinterpreting how they should distribute their attention as they move through the exhibition. Nonsystematic sequences of viewing exhibits often results in unintentionally missing exhibit elements and a failure to understand ideas that logically build from one exhibit element to another.

Decision-making Processes

Choice strongly characterizes visitor behavior within an exhibition. Visitors choose to stop or not stop at an exhibit, to examine it carefully or not, and to read interpretative materials or not. The economic concept of value provides a useful way to examine these choices.

1. **The value ratio.** The attention-value model asserts that the major motivation of paying attention to an exhibit is determined by the ratio of utility (benefits, satisfaction) divided by costs (time, effort) derived from the experience of engaging with an exhibit display or element. Chapters 6 through 8 provide evidence for the power of the value ratio in engaging attention.
2. **Utility** refers to the perceived or real benefit and/or satisfaction obtained by viewing or engaging with the exhibit. Utility may be predicted by the following:
    a. **Interest level.** Self-reported interest level may be one of the most important indicators of perceived benefit or utility.
    b. **Preknowledge.** Preknowledge is generally associated with interest level and ease of comprehension (workload).
    c. **Agenda.** The concept of "agenda" is one with much surplus meaning. It seems to include a combination of general factors (plan of how the visit will take place), other person factors from what visitors bring to their visit, and factors related to a specific visit (e.g., time budget, group goals). Nevertheless, previsit agendas are an important aspect of the satisfaction and benefits derived from a museum visit.
3. **Cost** encompasses the time, effort, or other possible resources such as money that are necessary to "consume" the product (engage with the exhibit). Chapters 6 through 8 examine how cost (text passage length or film duration) influences engaged attention.
4. **Available-alternatives theorem.** The value of viewing a particular exhibit element is not absolute: it varies depending on the alternatives available at any moment. A visitor is likely to give attention to a moderately interesting object if it is the only object available to view. When additional, more attractive objects are available, the visitor will decrease attention to the original object. Of course, an important element of value is the cost; if the cost in terms of time and effort are substantially different for one object versus another, then the value and thus attention to these objects will be affected. This theorem explains why an object that is physically isolated from others receives more attention: there is no competition from which to choose. It also partially explains the film choice paradox described later in Chapter 6. Although people routinely sit through a two-hour movie at a cinema, they rarely spend more than a few minutes viewing film contained within an exhibition. In an exhibition, films are in

competition with other attractive exhibit elements to view, and visitors are reluctant to invest a long time period to view a film when there are lower-cost exhibit element alternatives available.

5. **Small-cost theorem.** People tend to choose a low-cost alternative that may have a lower benefit over a higher-cost alternative with a higher benefit. Chapter 6 reports on a study in which respondents made choices between sets of two films, one always rated lower quality but of shorter duration, and the other rated higher quality but of longer duration. When the films were short (5 to 10 minutes), the higher-quality (and longer) film was chosen about 80 percent of the time. However, when the films were longer (40 to 80 minutes), the choices were reversed: the lower-quality, shorter 40-minute film was the overwhelming choice. Chapter 7 systematically replicates the findings of Chapter 6 in a study of engaged reading of text passages rather than film choices. These studies suggest that people may be more sensitive to the cost than to the benefits of available choices, all other factors being equal. If this finding holds up under future research, it provides further support for the notion that it is better to offer several low-cost, small-benefit choices than one high-cost choice with high benefit/utility.

Another example of the small cost theorem comes from one of my studies with Don Patterson (Bitgood & Patterson, 1993), in which an interpretive label of 150 words was divided into three labels of 50 words each. The percentage of readers more than doubled with the shorter labels. The workload of 50 words seems to encourage more persistent reading than the one of 150 words.

Physical and Mental States

There are several temporary states that either increase or decrease attention level (Bitgood, 2009a, 2009b, 2009c), probably by influencing the level of both utility and costs. The focus is often on those that decrease attention (fatigue, satiation), but there are other temporary states that increase the level of attention (curiosity, excitement). There seems to be very little research that explicitly examines the states that increase attention levels.[1] Curiosity and excitement about the content area are often mentioned as important to the visitor experience (e.g., Rounds, 2004), but have not been systematically studied objectively in museums as an independent variable (i.e., one that influences behavior outcomes). These are areas worthy of additional research. Physical and mental states include:

1. **Energy level.** People's energy level varies considerably depending upon amount of sleep, stress, illness, age, and so forth. When visitors have low

energy levels (for whatever reason), they are likely to pay attention to exhibits at a lower level than otherwise might be found. A distinction should be made between acute and chronic low energy. Museums can often reduce acute problems by designing the visitor experience. Chronic conditions require medical intervention.

2. **Fatigue.** Both physical and mental acute fatigue are possible during a museum visit. The concern here is for acute fatigue resulting from prolonged physical and/or mental exertion occurring during the museum visit. If the total time of the visit is long, physical fatigue is likely to occur. If the content of an exhibition is difficult to understand or is burdened with excessive information, mental fatigue may occur.

3. **Object satiation.** Object satiation occurs when a normally desirable experience is too homogenous or repetitive in its nature. You may enjoy viewing the vast variety of seashells found in the sea, but, after viewing many of similar size, shape, color, and texture, you are likely to become satiated (at least for a short time).

4. **Positive emotional states.** While fatigue, energy level, and satiation are phenomena that decrease the level of attention to exhibits, there are other states that increase attention. Visitor curiosity and excitement are two emotional states that museums often attempt to stimulate. Emotional states are a product of both what visitors bring to the museum (personal variables) and the on-site experience with exhibitions and programs (setting variables).

Physical and mental states appear to influence value: for example, when you have a low energy level, the perceived cost is higher than when you have a high energy level. In one of my studies with Renee Burt and Stephanie Dukes (Bitgood, Burt, & Dukes, 2010), we found that energy level ratings during the task correlated with the proportion of a text passage read.

Strategies and Learned Behavior Patterns

In addition to the psychological processes associated with detection, value, searching, and temporary states, there are strategies and learned behavior patterns that have an impact on visitor attention.

1. **Reading habits.** The pattern of starting to read the top paragraph on a page, then reading the one below in an top-to-bottom sequence seems to transfer to exhibit viewing (Bitgood & New, 2012). There is also the habit of starting at the left and moving to the right.

2. **Walking norms.** In the United States and many other countries, people tend to walk on the right side of a pathway, while countries that drive

on the left side apparently have a weaker tendency for this cultural norm. Walking on the right side of a pathway is likely to result in more attention to exhibit displays on the right side than to those on the left side.

3. **Previsit agenda.** This is a plan or strategy for the museum visit. The agenda may include viewing all of the exhibitions or viewing only a few, reading only identifying labels or trying to read all of the interpretive panels provided, taking a break to eat at the café or skipping lunch and eating an early dinner at home, etc. The agenda may have common elements from visit to visit, but it may also vary depending on time budget, group composition, etc. Agendas also change as visitors encounter the museum setting.

Part of an agenda may be a museum-visit script. A script is a typical sequence of events as part of the schema for common situations. We have scripts for visiting a restaurant or a doctor's office or any other common event in our lives. Scripts may differ from person to person. For example, visiting a museum for some families may mean purchasing something in the museum store, but for other families skipping the store to save money is part of their routine.

1. **Persistence.** Humans appear to have a strong tendency to persist at a task under certain conditions. Eisenberger (1985) reviewed the literature that showed when people are rewarded for effortful behavior, it generalizes to other behaviors; he called this "learned industriousness."
2. Chapters 9 and 10 report two studies that demonstrated people will read a larger proportion of a text passage if they were first instructed to describe or compare artworks before seeing the text passage. Chapter 11 reviews the use of handouts or guides in museums as a way to prompt more persistent attention to exhibit objects and interpretive information.

Concluding Comments

The attention-value model differs from other approaches in several ways:

1. It organizes the research findings and concepts somewhat differently than other approaches to visitor studies. Instead of an emphasis on the inferred outcome of learning, the model focuses on the impact of person-setting variables (e.g., interest, agendas, exhibit design) on paying attention. Managing visitor attention is what ultimately leads to learning, inquiry, and other inferred outcomes. Moreover, how attention is managed is likely to result in different types of inferred outcomes. For example, exhibits that are designed to create a feeling of time and place are likely to stimulate feelings and expressions of immersion, while a

hands-on science center device is more likely to create a cognitive understanding of a scientific principle.

2. The attention-value model emphasizes variables that have not often been studied. The predictive power of the value ratio (benefit-cost ratio) has not been explicitly applied to visitor attention in the past. Visitor studies have also neglected how visitors sequence their attention from one exhibit element to another within an exhibit display. The importance of movement or circulation patterns on visitor attention has received limited attention (Bitgood, 2006). While attention has received considerable mention in the literature, a model that encompasses all the important aspects of attention has not.

3. The model offers a comprehensive approach to managing attention that is both analytic and diagnostic. It is analytic in that it provides a comprehensive model of how psychological phenomena (decision-making, sensory perception, motivation) influence how visitors respond to exhibitions. It is diagnostic in that it provides a framework for applying key principles of managing attention, which should lead to inferred outcomes (e.g., learning) that require engaged attention.

4. The model also points to areas in need of further study (e.g., patterns of visual searching, the implications of the value ratio in decision-making, the influence of phenomena such as satiation and fatigue that interfere with paying attention, and the relationship between engaged attention and learning).

The remaining chapters provide evidence for the attention-value model (Chapters 6–14), review phenomena that decrease the level of attention (Chapter 15), and apply the attention value model to exhibit design principles (Chapters 16 and 17).

NOTES

The contents of this chapter are based primarily on two previous publications: Bitgood (2010) and Bitgood (2011a).

1. My students and I have collected data on self-reports of energy level, fatigue, interest, and satisfaction. Some of this data is reported in my book *Social Design in Museums: The Psychology of Visitor Studies*, Vol. 1 (2011a).

PART 2

Understanding Value and Motivation

chapter 6

Value as a Combination of Quality and Duration: Impact on Choice of Film

▹ **KEY IDEAS** ◃

- Value as a ratio of utility divided by cost has many applications, including choice of video or film embedded within exhibitions.
- To demonstrate that both utility (quality of film) and cost (film duration or run time) influence choice, a film festival scenario offered film choices that varied in both quality and duration.
- When given a choice between a higher-quality, longer-duration film and a lower-quality, shorter-duration film, individuals are sensitive to a combination of quality and duration.
- When films are relatively short (5 to 20 minutes), higher-quality, longer films are chosen more often; however, when film choices are long (more than 40 minutes), people choose the shorter, lower-quality film.
- Value is not fixed, as evidenced by the fact that selection of high quality (utility) depends on the time invested (film duration).
- The available-alternative theorem is supported by the findings: choice depends on the alternatives available at any moment.

Introduction

My attention-value model (Bitgood, 2010, 2011a; Chapter 5) suggests that engaged or deeply involved attention to something in the environment depends upon at least three conditions:

1. An individual's attention to an object must be captured and narrowly focused while attention to other objects is inhibited.
2. The object receiving attention must have a large perceived value to the individual, as measured by a ratio of utility divided by costs. Utility

Attention and Value: Keys to Understanding Museum Visitors by Stephen Bitgood, 77–82.

involves perceiving some level of satisfaction, benefit, or reward associated with the choice. Cost includes time, effort, or money required. Longer viewing time and more effort to "get the message" will decrease value and result in lower levels of attention.

3. **The available-alternatives theorem.** As described in Chapter 5, the alternative choices competing for attention at any moment must have a lower or equal perceived value ratio compared with the alternative actually chosen. In other words, the value of a choice must be considered relative to the value of available alternatives. *Value is not a constant, since it varies with the available choices at any moment.* If the choice is between a high- and medium-quality object, the choice will be the high-quality one; but if the choice is between a medium- versus low-quality object, then the medium-quality one will be selected.

More on the Available-Alternatives Theorem

To understand how attention is distributed to exhibit elements in an exhibition, we must consider further the alternatives available at any moment. In the early days of television, viewers were pleased to have two or three choices of shows to watch and often had no programming at all. Today, with hundreds of channels available on cable, satellite, and streaming video, hyperchoice is a serious problem. Channel surfing is symptomatic of decision-making behavior under multialternative conditions. A television show that was eagerly viewed 50 years ago may have less appeal today because there are so many alternatives available, many of which are targeted to special-interest audiences. More relevant to the current study, viewers will sit through a two-hour movie at the cinema, but will typically view a film imbedded within a museum exhibition for less than two or three minutes (e.g., Serrell, 2002). It is unlikely that this paradox is exclusively due to film quality. The availability of alternative attractions to view in the museum is undoubtedly a powerful factor.

The Film Festival Scenario and Video Viewing in Museums

Making choices among various alternatives available at any moment is common in our everyday life. At a three-day film festival, I found myself choosing a series of short films at one venue rather than a full-length film at a second venue. The short films offered lower costs (time) per film, and an expectation that at least one or two of the films would deliver high quality and would better address my personal interests; the long film, on the other hand, was a gamble in terms of quality and/or interest, and had a high cost in terms of viewing time. (See probability discounting for a similar pattern of choice [Greene & Myerson, 2004].)

Reflecting on the movie paradox of willingness to sit through a two-hour film at the cinema, but not view a film within an exhibition for more than a couple of minutes, there may be several factors that play a role:

1. **The potential quality of the film** (the "utility" or numerator in the value ratio). A film perceived as having higher quality would have greater value. One might assume that films in movie theaters are generally perceived as having higher interest and quality than those in museums.
2. **The duration of the film** (the "cost" or the denominator in the value ratio). According to the value ratio, increasing cost will decrease value. Since the film duration represents a cost to the viewer, longer films would have a lower value than shorter ones, all other factors being equal.
3. **The relative attractiveness or perceived value of alternative choices** (the available-alternatives theorem). The attention-value model predicts that choice depends upon the value of each available alternative.
4. **Commitment** (paying the ticket price and budgeting the time to sit in the theater reduces the chance of leaving the movie theater early). Museum visitors walking through a museum exhibition rarely commit themselves to view an entire video/film because of the competing exhibit elements around them. (See Rachlin & Green [1972] for a discussion of the "soft" versus "hard" commitment and laboratory studies demonstrating commitment.)
5. **A phenomenon similar to "commitment" called "sunk costs" is also likely to be a factor** (e.g., Arkes & Blumer, 1985). Once they have paid the entrance fee and settle in a comfortable seat, people are committed to stay and reluctant to leave a movie in a theater even if it is perceived as poor because they "want to get their money's worth."

Only the first three of the above factors were tested in our study. Commitment and sunk costs will be examined in future studies. This study assessed the impact of simultaneously varying the film quality (high, medium, or low) and length (from 5 to 80 minutes). Each pair of choices contrasts a shorter, lower-quality film with a longer, higher-quality film.

In addition to examining quality and duration variables, this study examined the *available-alternatives theorem*. If value is fixed, then participants would choose a high-quality film whether it has a low- or medium-quality alternative and whether the workload was high or low. We predicted that a high-quality, longer film will be chosen over a lower-quality film when the film is shorter (e.g., 5 to 10 minutes), but not when it is longer (40 to 80 minutes). The theorem predicts that the value (and consequently the choice) changes depending on both the quality and duration of the alternative. The study used a methodology similar to those used in studies of temporal discounting (Critchfield & Kollins, 2001) and consumer loyalty programs (e.g., Kivetz, 2003).

Method

Participants

Sixty-five undergraduate students from two psychology classes were given extra credit for volunteering for the study. Participants' ages ranged from 18 to 36 years, with most in the 18- to 21-year range.

Procedure

The participants were given extra credit for participating in a study involving decision-making. Participation was voluntary, and students who did not want to take part could either sit quietly or leave the classroom. All students remained and participated in the task.

Participants were presented with the following scenario:

> You are attending a film festival with two venues (choices) per time slot and you must choose between the two. One film will always be a shorter, lower-quality film and the other a longer, higher-quality film. The duration of the films will vary from 5 to 80 minutes and the quality of film will vary from low to medium to high as rated by a panel of film experts.

The study was conducted at the end of a class period and was completed in less than 30 minutes. A total of 21 pairs of choices were displayed on an overhead projector. Length of the second alternative choice in each pair was always twice that of the first choice (e.g., 5 versus 10 minutes, 10 versus 20 minutes, 15 versus 30 minutes, etc.). Examples of choices were as follows:

1. 10-minute low-quality film versus a 20-minute medium-quality film
2. 30-minute medium-quality film versus a 60-minute high-quality film
3. 40-minute low-quality film versus an 80-minute high-quality film

Results

Table 6.1 contains the percentage of choices for the longer, higher-rated film for three of the seven film-duration comparisons.[1] Two general outcomes are evident:

1. At shorter durations (5 versus 10 minutes), the higher-rated, 10-minute film had a high probability of being selected (84.6 to 94.2 percent); however, with the longest films (40 versus 80 minutes), fewer respondents chose the higher-rated film (19.2 to 36.5 percent of the time).
2. The higher-quality film was more likely to be selected when there is a larger contrast in quality (i.e., high versus low) than when the contrast is low (low versus medium or medium versus high).

Table 6.1: Percentage Choosing the Longer, Higher-Rated Film for Combinations of Duration Pairs and Quality Differences

	Quality Difference, %		
Time Pair, min	Low-Medium	Medium-High	Low-High
5–10	84.6	84.6	94.2
20–40	36.5	38.5	86.5
40–80	23.1	19.2	36.5

Note: Statistical comparisons with Chi square show highly significant differences for the contrast effects between low-high and the low-medium or medium-high pairs at the 20- to 40-minute and 40- to 80-minute film durations, but not at the 5- to 10-minute durations.

Discussion

This study found that quality, costs (duration of film), and characteristics of alternative choices are all important when considering why people are willing to engage their attention on a film.

Selection of the higher-quality film was strongly influenced by the cost (film duration). When the cost (5 to 10 minutes) was low, participants chose the longer, higher-quality film about 85 to 95 percent of the time. When the cost was high (40 to 80 minutes), the shorter, lower-quality film was the dominant choice. Other factors being equal, this outcome suggests that no matter what the quality of the film, there are limits to what types of costs the audience will tolerate. There is always a trade-off between quality and costs. At some point, people settle for lower quality if the price (cost) is right.

Available-Alternative Theorem

The study also found that the alternative choices available at any moment are of critical importance in decision-making. When there was a small difference in quality (e.g., low-medium or medium-high), the shorter, lower-quality film had the advantage. However, when the quality difference was large (e.g., low-high), the longer, higher-quality film had a greater chance of being chosen.

Two conclusions can be drawn from this study: (1) higher-quality experiences are preferred when the cost is reasonably low, but choice is reversed when the cost (duration of film) is high; and (2) higher-quality films have a larger value when the contrast in quality between alternatives is perceived to be high (low versus high).

Conclusion

If the findings of this study generalize to exhibitions (which I believe they do), it suggests that the choice of paying attention to various exhibit elements depends upon the perceived value of each exhibit element available at any moment. When there are competing exhibit objects/elements, those with high utility (e.g., perceived interest) and low cost (time, effort) are most likely to be given attention. Further, the probability of paying attention to any exhibit element varies depending on the contrasting value of other available exhibit elements. When attempting to design an exhibition that successfully manages visitor attention, the relationship among exhibit displays and elements must be considered.

The next chapter provides further evidence of the impact of value. The Chapter 7 study shows how the benefits and costs of text material jokes and weather information influence choice of which of two passages to read.

NOTES

This chapter is based on Bitgood, New, & Abby (2011).

1. To minimize confusion, only three of the seven film-duration pairs are presented in Table 6.1. The remaining data show a similar pattern.

chapter 7

How Value Influences Choice of Text Passages

▷ **KEY IDEAS** ◁

- The value ratio (quality divided by workload) can be applied in many ways, including how visitors choose (or do not choose) to read exhibit text in exhibition centers.
- The study in this chapter demonstrates how both utility, as measured by quality of text content, and cost, as measured by total words available to read (workload), influence choice of how much to read.
- When cost (or workload) is high, individuals are willing to settle for lower-quality content. This suggests value is sensitive to cost and that it is important to keep time and effort at a minimum.

Introduction

There are studies in marketing, economics, and psychology that support the notion that choice depends upon value, defined as a combination of utility (benefit) and the costs (time, effort) required to obtain the benefit. These studies include temporal discounting (e.g., Critchfield & Kollins, 2001), optimal foraging theory (e.g., Pirolli & Card, 1999), and loyalty programs (e.g., Kivetz, 2003). Defining value as a ratio of utility to cost is the basis of behavioral economics (e.g., Wilkinson, 2008).

The previous chapter demonstrated that value (defined as a combination of benefits and costs) influences choice between pairs of films. In this chapter, we apply the value principle to text passages. It is well documented that museum visitors are more likely to read short rather than long text passages (e.g., Bitgood, 1989, 2000, 2002; Screven, 1992; Serrell, 1996). However, there are times when short passages are ignored and longer passages are read. The attention-value model explains this inconsistency by assuming that both the perceived utility (benefits, satisfaction) and the costs (time, effort, money)

Attention and Value: Keys to Understanding Museum Visitors by Stephen Bitgood, 83–91.

combine to influence the choice of reading or not reading text. If perceived utility is high enough, visitors will read longer text passages even if the workload is moderately high. However, there are limits: if the perceived cost is too high, visitors engage in little or no reading.

Museum visitors consider perceived benefit when choosing to read or not read exhibit labels/text. It is difficult (although not impossible) to accurately measure this judgment process during a museum visit. One way to study perceived utility and costs in the decision-making process is to make it more explicit in a simulation study. For example, if participants are given information about the quality of information as well as the workload (time and effort required), we should be able to more accurately assess the impact of differences in perceived benefits and costs between two text passages. The two studies I discuss in this chapter assigned judgments of quality to text passages and examined the choice behavior of participants when quality and workload simultaneously varied over the course of the study. That is, on any trial, quality of the information varied among high, medium, or low and number of words (workload) varied between 25 and 200 in the first study and between 25 and 600 in the second. For example, participants might be offered the choice of reading a 25-word text passage rated as low quality versus a 50-word text passage with a high-quality rating. The question: How much effort are people willing to expend given each level of quality? At some point, it may not be worth the effort, even if the perceived payoff is large. I believe the results help explain how museum visitors choose to read text passages in exhibits.

In addition to examining the actual workload (total words in the text passage), I was concerned with how people perceive workload. If individuals are only given the number of words in a text passage, is that equivalent to actually seeing the text passage in its full length? Seeing the length of the passage is what visitors experience in museums. It remains to be demonstrated if knowing the number of words results in the same judgment of workload as seeing the entire passage.

The studies in this chapter examine choice of text passages based on both the perceived utility (quality of information) and the cost (length of text passage required to read). Participants were given a series of choices in which one choice was always a lower-quality/shorter passage (e.g., 25 words/low quality) and the other was always a higher-quality/longer passage (e.g., 50 words/medium quality). The first study also compared the way information is delivered to individuals. Information about the length of the passage was presented in one of three forms (visual, written, or verbal) to three separate groups.

Study 1

In this study, we varied utility (benefit) and costs. To ensure relatively high interest, we selected humor or jokes as the content of text passages. We reasoned that jokes are likely to have more general appeal and be consistently more motivating to participants than other topics. Assuming that higher-quality jokes have greater appeal than lower quality, utility was divided into three levels of quality: high, medium, and low. The number of words in the text passage was considered a cost or "workload" factor.

We might question how people make their judgments of possible costs and benefits when confronted by a text passage. Consider the costs. Obviously, visitors do not consciously count the number of words before deciding whether or not to read. It is more likely that people have an intuitive grasp of the length of a text passage and how much work it requires to read it, even though they may not be accurate at estimating the number of words by simply glancing at the passage. In the first study, we compared three methods of presenting the choices. The purpose was to identify conditions that were most sensitive to utility-cost manipulations.

Utility may be difficult to measure or manipulate because it differs from individual to individual. The study attempted to avoid this problem by manipulating utility with the assignment of a quality rating (high, medium, or low) to the jokes. The quality ratings were based on an independent group's rating.

Participants were asked to choose between jokes of varying length and of differing quality (high, medium, low). Each trial consisted of a choice between a shorter-length, lower-quality joke and a longer-length, higher-quality joke. The workload or number of words varied from 25 versus 50, 50 versus 100, and 100 versus 200.

Method

PARTICIPANTS. A total of 60 undergraduate students from Jacksonville State University participated in this study during the fall semester of 2006. Students were given extra credit in the class from which they were recruited. They were told that the purpose of the study was to examine decision-making about the quality of jokes.

MATERIALS. Jokes were gathered from Internet searches and modified by either adding filler words or by taking away words to control the specific number of words. The length of jokes was 25, 50, 100, or 200 words. After the modification, these jokes were given to a different class of 60 students via an overhead projector; students were asked to rate the quality of jokes on a 10-point scale. Based on student ratings, the jokes were classified as low, medium, or high quality. A total of 36 jokes were selected from the original pool for the study: two jokes in each combination of word total and quality (e.g., 25-low/50-medium; 25-low/50-high).

Participants were seated, one at a time, at a table across from one of the experimenters. The following introduction was read to all participants:

> The purpose of this experiment is to see how you make decisions concerning the quality of jokes. On each trial, two jokes will be presented in front of you. The left side joke will always be the shorter one. The right side joke will be longer but has been rated as funnier by a group of students. Your job is to choose one of the jokes, read it and tell us if you agree with the previous rating of how funny it is. Do not attempt to plan ahead. Please judge each choice based on which one is most appealing to you. After selecting one of the jokes, please read it out loud and rate it as either high, medium, or low in terms of how funny it is.

PROCEDURES. A total of 18 pairs of jokes (36 total) were used in the study. Participants were instructed to choose one of two jokes for each set, one always with fewer words and a lower-quality rating and the other with more words and a higher-quality rating. After the selection, the participant was asked to read the joke out loud. Finally, the participant was asked to rate the quality of the joke.

The participants were divided into the following three experimental conditions:

1. **Visual presentation.** A group of 21 students were shown two 6-inch x 9-inch cards with jokes ranging from 25 to 200 words visible to the student. The top of each card also identified the quality of the joke (high, medium, or low).
2. **Written presentation.** A group of 19 students served in this condition. Two 6-inch x 9-inch cards were presented to students. Each card had the rating of joke quality (high, medium, low) and the number of words for the joke. The actual text of the joke was not visible until participants made their choice. After the participant made a selection, a card with the text of the joke was presented and the participant was asked to read the joke out loud.
3. **Verbal presentation.** The last group of 20 students was not given written or visual descriptions of the jokes. Instead, they were asked if they would prefer to read a lower-rated joke with fewer words (e.g., a low-rated, 25-word joke) or a higher-rated joke with more words (e.g., a high-

rated, 50-word joke). After making a choice, participants were shown the joke and asked to read out loud.

Results and Discussion

Table 7.1 summarizes the percentages of participants who chose the longer, higher-rated joke in each of the conditions across increasing text length. Clearly, the visual presentation condition displayed more sensitivity to the different choices. More than 68 percent chose the 50-word, higher-quality joke over the 25-word, lower-quality joke; when the choice was between 50 and 100 words, only 49.2 percent selected the higher-quality joke; and when the choice was between 100 and 200 words, only 38.9 percent chose the longer/higher-quality one.

Neither the written nor the verbal conditions showed as much variation in choice across word length increases as in the visual condition. In the written condition, only the 100- to 200-word choice resulted in a marked decrease (49.0 percent) compared with more than 70 percent for the 25- to 50-word and 50- to 100-word lengths. In the verbal condition, there was little difference in choosing the longer, higher-rated joke across the three word-length intervals.

The findings in Table 7.1 also reveal that seeing the text passage (visual condition) resulted in the lowest numbers choosing the longer, higher-rated joke in all three word comparisons (25 to 50, 50 to 100, and 100 to 200). This suggests that visual perception of workload is perceived to be a higher cost than knowing the actual number of words (written and verbal conditions). Seeing the passage is not equivalent to knowing the number of words.

Table 7.1: Percentages of Participants Choosing the Longer, Higher-rated Joke

Condition	25-50 word	50-100 word	100-200 word
Visual	68.3	49.2	38.9
Written	72.9	72.0	49.0
Verbal	76.5	72.0	68.9

Note: Statistical analysis of data shows that conditions (visual versus written versus verbal conditions) were significantly different, as were effort comparisons (25 to 50 versus 50 to 100 versus 100 200 words).

Table 7.2 shows the percentage of individuals (for the visual presentation condition) who chose the longer/higher-rated joke for the three comparisons (low-medium, medium-high, and low-high). Note that in the low-high comparison, participants were more likely to choose the higher-quality joke than in the low-medium or medium-high comparison. Individuals appear to be sensitive to the quality differences: when there is a large difference (low-high), participants are likely to choose higher quality than when there is a smaller difference (low-medium, medium high).

The results of the study show that when choosing to read text passages, people are sensitive to both the quality of information and the workload involved. However, the method of presentation is important. The visual presentation format was shown to be most sensitive to the independent variables (showed a larger difference among the three word comparisons) and was apparently perceived as a larger workload than simply knowing the number of words. The visual condition format is more similar to the task of actual museum visitors than is the written or verbal condition format.

Table 7.2: Percentage of Participants Choosing the Longer, Higher-quality Joke in the Visual Presentation

Effort Comparison	Low-Medium	Medium-High	Low-High
25 vs 50 words	66.7	64.3	73.8
50 vs 100 words	50.0	38.1	59.5
100 vs 200 words	33.3	40.5	42.9

The workload difference (25 versus 50 words, 50 versus 100 words, and 100 versus 200 words) may have been too small a difference to show a large impact on the workload factor. Thus, in the next study, the workload difference was expanded from two times the first value (e.g., 25 to 50), to three times (e.g., 25 to 75).

Study 2

The first study established that quality (an indicator of utility) and workload (an indicator of cost) combine to influence choice of which text passage to read. However, a couple of questions can be raised: Does this effect apply only to information likely to be interesting, such as jokes? Do participants actually have to read the text passages for the effect to occur, or would we get similar choice results if participants made their choices between pairs of passages, but did not have to actually read them? This question is at the heart of the validity of simulation studies. There is always concern about the experiential realism of simulation studies.

Utility was examined in the first study by assigning quality (high, medium, or low) to the text passages. Another way to study utility is to offer text content that differs in terms of interest. In the second study we added text passages on weather; it is assumed that jokes have a higher inherent interest than weather as a topic. As will be shown, this assumption was supported by the findings: the choice of high-quality weather passages was lower than for high-quality jokes.

While the quality differences were similar to Study 1 (low, medium, or high), the workload differences between choices were increased to 25 to 75 words, 50 to 150 words, 100 to 300 words, and 200 to 600 words. The failure to find a large choice difference in the written and verbal conditions when the workload was twice as much in the second choice than in the first may be because of low contrast between workload choices.

The greater differences in workload choice in this study helped to test the available-alternative theorem (i.e., value is not absolute; it is based on the alternatives available at the moment). This theorem predicts that the choice of a higher-quality text passage will depend on the relative workloads (text passage length) and the quality contrast between alternatives (i.e., low-high versus medium-high).

Method

The method was similar to that used in Study 1 with three exceptions. First, weather was added to jokes as a second topic of information. In addition, workload differences between the shorter, lower-rated passage and the longer, higher-rated passage were increased to three times rather than two used in the first study. Finally, participants made choices between text differences of different quality and length, but, unlike the first study, did not actually read the passage after making their choice. Thus, the workload (reading) was symbolic rather than experiential.

Results and Discussion

Table 7.3 summarizes the results for Study 2. The important findings include:

1. Higher-quality passages were preferred when the workload (effort) was low, but lower-quality passages were preferred when the effort (i.e., longer passages) was high (200 to 600 words).
2. The available-alternative theorem was demonstrated in comparing choices between medium- and high-quality and low- and high-quality passages. The high-quality passage was more likely to be selected when

the alternative was low than when it was medium. The contrast between high and low quality is greater than between high and medium quality.
3. Choice was also influenced by the content (jokes versus weather). High-quality jokes were selected at a higher percentage over medium- or lower-quality jokes compared with weather passages. This suggests that jokes are of greater interest/satisfaction than weather reports; this difference is indicated by how often higher-quality passages are selected.

Table 7.3: Percentage of Respondents Choosing the Higher-quality/Longer Text Passage

		Quality Differences, %		
Type of Info	**Comparison**	**Low-Med**	**Med-high**	**Low-High**
Jokes	25-75 words	81.8	90.9	90.9
	50-150 words	69.7	81.3	93.9
	100-300 words	69.7	66.7	75.8
	200-600 words	36.4	42.4	63.6
Weather	25-75 words	75.8	78.8	78.8
	50-150 words	54.6	27.3	75.8
	100-300 words	42.4	33.3	51.5
	200-600 words	27.3	15.2	36.4

General Discussion

Study 1 found that choice of text passages was sensitive to the quality-workload values when the entire text was presented to individuals. Study 2 found a similar impact of quality-workload combinations whether the subject matter was jokes or weather. The specific type of information may influence level of value, but not the basic pattern of choice.

As predicted by the attention-value model, value (as indicated by the reading choice) was influenced by both quality of information and by workload. The Chapter 6 study showed that value (as measured by quality divided by time of film) predicted film-viewing choices. This finding seems to generalize to text passages of other subject matters (humor and weather).

Choices were independent of actual workload: participants tended to show the same pattern of choice whether or not they had to read the passages they selected. This suggests that simulation studies can give us valid predictions of decision-making in the "real" world.

Finally, we can argue that the level of utility is not fixed or absolute; it varies with the value of choices as predicted by the available-alternative theorem. What is chosen in one situation may not be chosen when the context changes. Low quality is more likely to be chosen if the contrasting alternative is of medium rather than of high quality; higher quality is more likely to be chosen when the workload is low.

How does this apply to museums? Visitors are constantly choosing whether or not to pay attention. The ratio of benefits (utility, satisfaction) to cost (time, effort) is critical in this decision and should be carefully designed into the visitor experience. This can be accomplished by reducing the workload whenever possible by clear, concise writing, by avoiding exhibit layouts that require unnecessary cognitive processing, and by maximizing the utility (benefits) with high-interest content and provocative wording.

In addition, since choice varies with the available alternatives, the relationship among exhibit displays and elements must be considered. When visitors are given a choice between a high-value and a low-value alternative exhibit, they are likely to skip the low-value one. Careful layouts that minimize competition between exhibit elements of highly different values should be avoided.

Additional research is needed to determine the extent of influence of available alternatives. How close together do exhibit elements and displays have to be to be considered a viable alternative choice? How far apart must we place two blocks of text for them to be considered independent of one another in terms of choice?

NOTE

Adapted from Bitgood & Dukes (2011). Presented at the Southeastern Psychological Association, New Orleans, LA.

chapter 8

Predicting Engaged Attention to Exhibit Text Passages

▹ **KEY IDEAS** ◃

- According to the attention-value model, the value ratio can be expressed as a ratio of interest (utility) divided by workload or time and effort (cost).
- Three studies examine the impact of interest rating, workload (total words available in a passage), and the ratio of interest rating/workload on partial and deep levels of reading engagement.
- The value ratio (interest/workload) was the best predictor of reading. Workload was also highly correlated with reading.
- Interest may be most important to encourage some reading, but workload (cost) seems to be a more powerful factor in determining how much reading occurs.

Introduction

As indicated in previous chapters, the attention-value model argues that the third stage of attention (engagement) requires deep processing of information and that both benefits and costs combine to predict engaged attention. The previous two chapters examine the impact of benefit-cost combinations on choices between two alternatives at a time. This chapter also demonstrates how people make decisions when the benefits and costs vary. In this case, the amount of a text passage read related to artworks is examined when interest and workload (number of words available to read) are systematically changed.

Chapter 6 demonstrates that the choice of film depends upon both the quality of film and its duration. When film length is short, the higher-quality film is the overwhelming choice; however, when the film length is long, individuals are more likely to select the shorter, lower-quality film. The Chapter 7

Attention and Value: Keys to Understanding Museum Visitors by Stephen Bitgood, 92–107.

study found that the text passage length of the universally appealing subject of jokes and the less appealing subject of weather influences the choice of higher- versus lower-quality content. A lower-quality, shorter joke is more likely to be selected over a higher-quality, longer joke; however, when the text lengths are short, the higher-quality longer text is selected. In Chapters 6 and 7 I discussed the implications these results have for films and text within museum exhibitions. These findings support the argument that the value ratio, defined as benefit divided by cost, is significantly influenced by the cost (long text or films) as well as the benefit (viewing or reading high-quality film or text). The value of a choice is not constant and based only on the benefits; it changes with the costs. The economic concept of value has many applications in everyday decision-making in addition to what is usually thought of as "economics."

In this chapter, I examine the value ratio as a predictor of engaged reading about artworks. *Interest* in a topic is assumed to be an indicator of potential benefits while *workload* (a combination of time and effort required to process information) is assumed to represent the cost of engaged reading. The purpose of these studies is to examine more closely how the value ratio (benefits/costs) influences the processes of what is given attention. To what degree does high interest overcome high workload? Will people read long text passages if interest level is high enough? Or, does a high workload inhibit engaged reading of text passages despite high interest?

From the perspective of the attention-value model, the vast majority of advice on label design (e.g., Bitgood, 2000; Screven, 1992; Serrell, 1996) can be categorized into the two components of value: (1) the cost (time, effort) of reading and comprehending the material; and (2) the benefits (e.g., satisfaction, pursuing an interest, learning something new).

The Possible Cost of Reading

Reading text labels in exhibitions always has a cost (time and effort required to process information) that often go unrecognized by developers and designers. These costs include:

1. **Workload:** the amount of reading (i.e., the total number of words), which indicates the time and effort required to process information.
2. **Ease of processing information:** difficult vocabulary and sentence structure make cognitive processing more difficult, contributing to cost.
3. **Placement of text material:** the proximity of the text material to the object being described. The greater the distance between an object and the label describing it, the greater the cost.
4. **Coding:** systems that require translating the relationship between objects and interpretive text (e.g., placing numbers on objects located

within an exhibit case that refer to text material on an interpretive panel usually outside the exhibit case).

5. **Layout of exhibit elements:** this refers to how elements are organized within the exhibit display influences cost. A well-designed layout of text and object elements reduces time and effort to process the information. For example, time and effort is reduced if text material is connected by a line to a specific location on an illustration.

The Possible Benefits of Reading

The benefits of reading are all closely related to personal interest and satisfaction obtained from reading text:

1. Satisfying curiosity regarding information about a high-interest topic.
2. Learning something new, giving meaning to an exhibit object, or confirming something you thought you knew.
3. Being provoked by a question or statement that makes you want to learn more.

This chapter reports on three museum simulation studies that examined the role of interest, workload, and the value ratio on engaged reading. A summary of some of the data contained in this chapter as well as other studies related to the attention-value model can be found in Bitgood (2011a, pp. 230–295).

Predictions of the Attention-Value Model

Using a path analysis, Figure 8.1 compares the attention-value model with other approaches with regard to value, interest, workload, and engaged attention. The top illustration indicates that interest and workload both contribute value, which in turn influences engaged attention. The bottom illustration ("Other Models") suggests a direct impact between interest and engaged attention, and workload and engaged attention instead of being mediated by value. The attention-value model argues that the value ratio will be a more powerful predictor of engaged attention than either interest or workload by itself.

The studies in this chapter are museum simulation studies. The purpose is to isolate the decision-making processes that people use both in museums and in making everyday choices. Simulation studies need to be validated by examining similar visitor reactions in museums. The studies conducted in our

Figure 8.1: Path Analysis for Concepts and Measures (The Attention-Value Model)

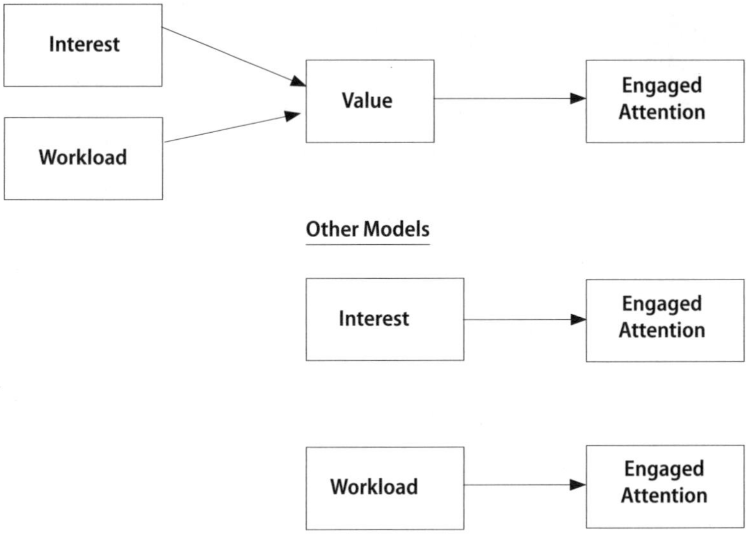

laboratory appear consistent with how visitors actually behave in museums with at least one major difference: the actual chances of reading are higher in the laboratory studies than in museums, presumably because participants are cued to read in the laboratory, but it is noteworthy that the amount of reading varies widely (as it does in museums). The choice of whether and how much to read is likely motivated by value in both the laboratory and the museum. Ultimately, studies similar to those in this chapter can be replicated in museum settings to validate the findings.

Study 1

Method

PARTICIPANTS. For all three studies discussed in this chapter, a total of 103 participants, 61 women and 42 men ranging in age from 18 to 36 years, were recruited from introductory psychology classes at Jacksonville State University during the spring and fall semesters of 2006. Students were given extra credit for their participation. Only three of the students majored or minored in art.

MATERIALS. Art prints by well-known artists (see lists in Tables 8.1–8.3) were used in the study. The prints were selected from Canaday's *The Metropolitan Seminars in Art* (1958) published by the Metropolitan Museum of Art. Content of the descriptive text passages was obtained from several sources in the art literature. The passages varied both in terms of number of words and, for Studies 2 and 3, for the number of bulleted points which varied from three to ten bulleted statements. For Study 1, the passages were in paragraph form. Sample passages can be found in Appendix A.

PROCEDURES. Participants were seated at a table across from the experimenter. The art prints were presented one at a time. The participant was instructed to examine the print and give a rating from 1 (lowest) to 10 (highest) indicating his/her level of interest in seeing information about the artwork and the artist. After recording the participant's interest rating, the experimenter turned over the print to reveal a text passage in bulleted format of varying lengths. Tables 8.1, 8.2, and 8.3 list the artists, artworks, and length of the passages for all three studies. In all three studies, participants were given a choice of reading none of the passage, reading some of the passage (as little or as much as desired), or reading all of the passage. Participants were instructed to read out loud. In the first study, the experimenter recorded if the participant read all, some, or none of the passage. In Studies 2 and 3, the experimenter checked each bulleted item as it was read. With only a few minor exceptions, participants tended to read an entire bulleted item once they started reading. They occasionally skipped some bulleted items, but tended to read an entire item or none of it.

RECALL. In Study 2, after recording the number of bulleted items read, the experimenter removed the art print and asked the participant to write down all the information recalled from the text passage. The content of information recalled was later scored for each bulleted point. Partial recall of information in a teaching point was counted if two independent recorders agreed that it was sufficient.

Table 8.1 compares the three studies in terms of number of participants, number of prints, range of text passage length, and reading measures. From this table it is evident that the range of the text passages differed among the three studies; the first study had the greatest range (149 to 315 words) and the fewest number of passages (nine) longer than 200 words. The second study had the largest number of passages (ten) shorter than 100 words.

Study 1: Results and Discussion

Figure 8.2 summarizes the strength of the relationships between each pair of terms (interest-value, workload-value, value-reading, interest-reading, and

Figure 8.2: Path Analysis Outcome for Study 1 (Complete Data)

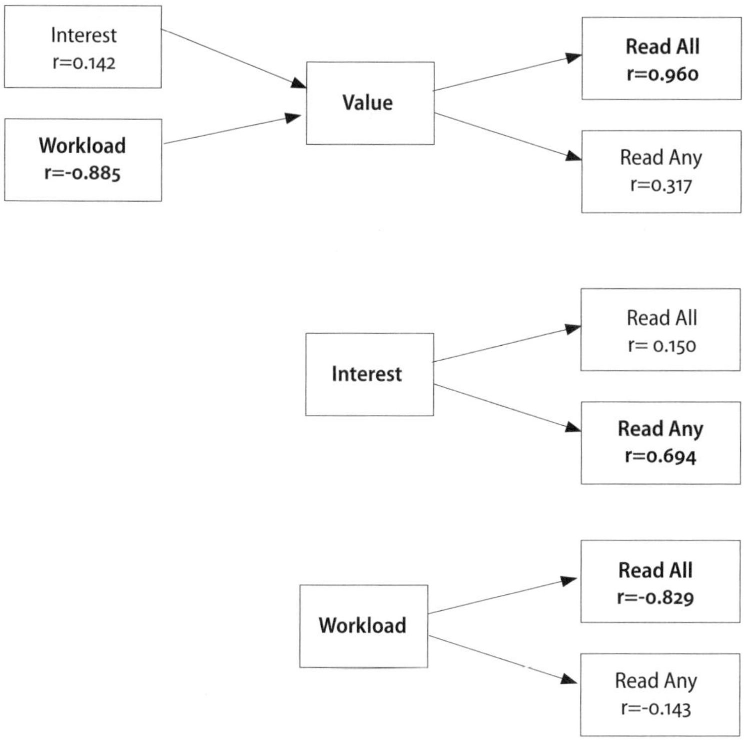

workload-reading). The greater the correlation (r value), the more powerful the prediction. A perfect correlation would be $r = 1.0$; generally, any value above 0.50 indicates a high correlation. The closer R is to 0, the lower the relationship between factors. Note that a negative correlation indicates that as one variable increases, the other decreases. Thus, as the number of words in a passage increases, the proportion of the passage actually read decreases.

VALUE. The workload-value correlation ($r = -0.885$) is considerably higher than the interest-value correlation ($r = 0.142$), suggesting that workload contributes more to value than does interest. In addition, value is highly predictive of the "read all" measure ($r = 0.960$), but not with the "read any" measure ($r = 0.317$). Value is an excellent predictor of "read all," but not "read any."

INTEREST. Interest is not a predictor of "read all" ($r = 0.150$), but is highly correlated with "read any" ($r = -0.694$). While interest did not predict reading the complete passage, it was a good predictor of reading some of it.

WORKLOAD. To a lesser extent than with value, workload is highly correlated with "read all" ($r = -0.829$), and poorly correlated with "read any" ($r = -0.143$). The negative correlation indicates that as workload increases, reading decreases.

Are there two kinds of engaged attention? The two measures of reading (read all and read any) were associated with different factors: "read all" with value and workload, and "read any" with interest. This suggests two levels of engaged attention: deeply engaged attention associated with reading all the text, and partially engaged attention indicated by reading any of the text.

INFLUENCE OF TEXT PASSAGE LENGTH. One of the concerns with Study 1 is the range of word length in the text passages. The wide range (49 to 315 words) is likely to have exaggerated the outcome in favor of workload influence. To address the possibility that long passages strongly influenced the outcome, we examined only those text passages that were less than 100 words. Does the pattern of correlations among the concepts change when only shorter passages are examined? Figure 8.3 provides the findings from the seven passages that contained fewer than 100 words. A comparison of Figures 8.2 and 8.3 reveals some similarities and several changes. First, the correlations between interest-value and workload-value are similar for both analyses of text passage length (the sample of passages shorter than 100 words and the entire range of passages). However, the value–"read any" correlation increased from r = 0.317 (for the full range of text passages) to r = 0.848 (for text passages under 100 words). Thus, for shorter passages, the value ratio was a strong predictor of both reading measures, while it was not strongly correlated with "read any" for the entire range of text passages.

The interest-read correlations also changed. With the shorter passages, the relationship between interest and "read any" was reduced (from $r = 0.694$ to 0.433). Workload-reading measure correlations also changed: the "read any" measure substantially increased from $r = -0.143$ to -0.876. The "read all" measures remained about the same from Figures 8.2 to 8.3.

Comparing both samples in the study (less than 100 words versus the complete range), it appears that interest is more sensitive to longer than shorter text passages. This is consistent with the notion that as the cost (workload) is kept to a minimum, high interest may not be required for engaged attention.

Study 2: Results and Discussion

Figure 8.4 summarizes the results of the second study. The pattern of correlations resembles, to a large extent, that found in Figure 8.3 from text passages of less than 100 words in Study 1:

Figure 8.3: Path Analysis Outcome for Study 1 (Passages Under 100 Words)

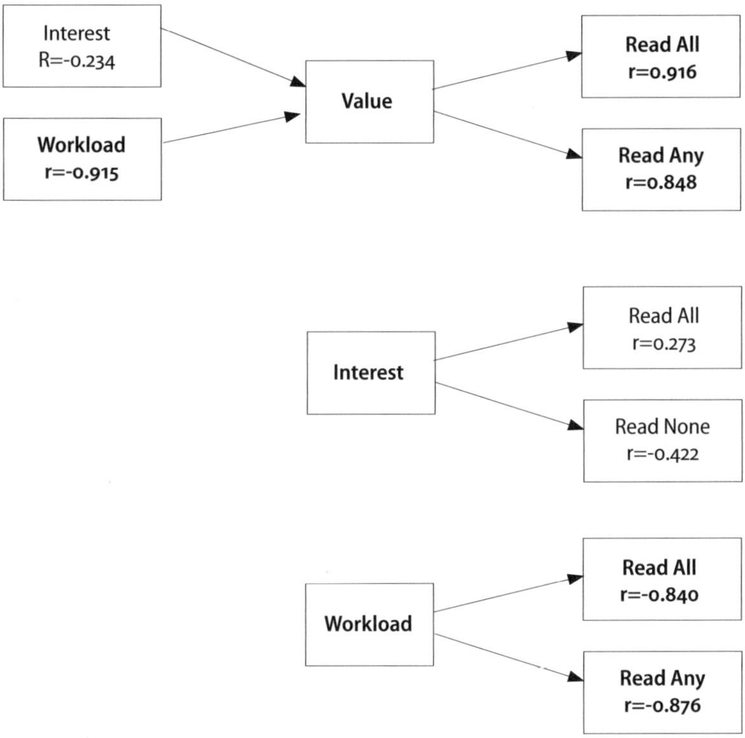

1. Workload is highly correlated with value, but interest is not.
2. Value is significantly correlated with both measures of reading.
3. Interest is not highly correlated with either reading measures.
4. Workload is highly correlated with both measures of reading.

CONCLUSION. Consistent with the shorter passages of Study 1 (see Figure 8.3), interest had less impact with shorter passages. When workload is low, interest is less of an issue than when workload is high.

Recall of text information was not improved by offering either longer text passages or by higher interest ratings. Recall was related only to how much of the text passage was read ($r = 0.810$). Increasing the length of the text passage did not increase the amount of information recalled. The more of the text passage that was read, the greater the recall.

Figure 8.4: Path Analysis Outcome for Study 2

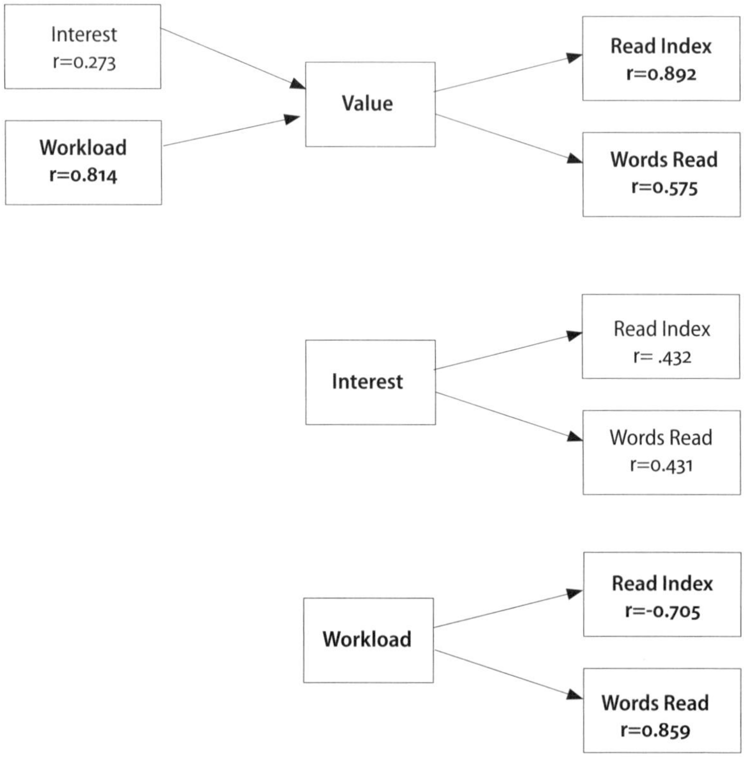

Study 3: Results and Discussion

Figure 8.5 summarizes the findings of Study 3. The pattern is similar to that of Study 1 (with the full range of passage length). Workload correlated more highly with value than with interest. Value predicted the reading index (proportion of passage read), while interest predicted total words read; finally, workload (similar to value) correlated with read index, but not words read.

CONCLUSION. When the range of text passages is great (62 to 215) and/or the average number of words per passage is high (e.g., 127.8 words for this study), interest has a larger impact when text passages are short (small workload). Interest influences number of words read, not the read index.

General Discussion

At first glance, the findings of these three studies may appear somewhat confusing. However, there is consistency across the three studies. The most

Figure 8.5: Path Analysis Outcome for Study 3

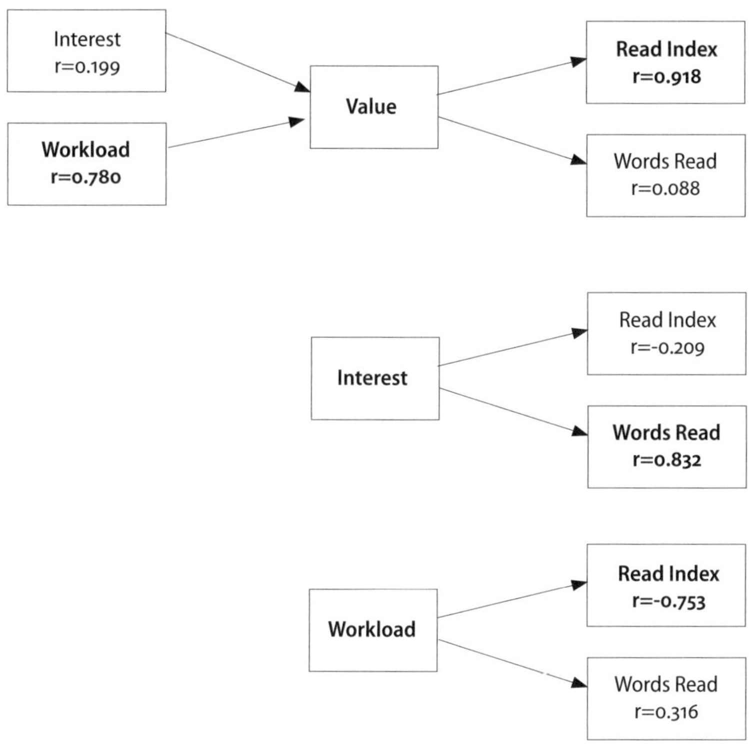

important finding was the difference between reading measures that take more time and effort (deeply engaged reading) from those that require less time and effort (partially engaged attention).

Deeply Engaged Reading

As predicted by the attention-value model, the value ratio was the best predictor of deeply engaged reading in all three studies. In addition, workload was also a strong predictor of engaged reading. Unexpectedly, interest rating was *not* highly correlated with deeply engaged reading as might be expected from traditional educational theories of interest (e.g., Ainley, Hidi, & Berndorff, 2002; Krapp & Prenzel, 2011; Linnenbrink-Garcia, et al., 2010).

Partially Engaged Reading

While interest rating was not correlated with deeply engaged reading, Studies 1 and 3 did find a high correlation between interest rating and partially engaged reading. Interest may become more important when the workload is high. Interest seems to motivate the reader to read at least some of a passage in the face of a heavy workload.

When the workload is low, people are more willing to read (even if interest level is low), presumably because the cost of investing time and effort is low and "worth a gamble." When the workload is high, people may be more sensitive to "loss aversion" as suggested by the prospect theory of Kahneman & Tversky (1979), who argued that decisions about chance are more sensitive to losses than to gains.

These conclusions are tentative. Further study is necessary to better understand the role of interest and how it relates to workload, value, and reading. Does interest motivate individuals to read more or to persevere when the workload is high? Are the concepts of personal and situational interest from educational psychology relevant to our analysis? How do concepts such as concreteness-abstractness play a role in exhibit label reading?

Whatever the mechanism, workload does appear to inhibit reading. The unpleasantness of high workload may trigger an avoidance reaction or "loss aversion." More research within the museum setting itself will hopefully shed light on the interrelationships among workload, interest, value, and reading of text material. While the findings of these studies are consistent with the attention-value model, more details of how these mechanisms work are needed.

The findings of this study do not rule out an important role for interest rating. Chapter 11 reports a study that demonstrates that people choose higher-interest objects (artwork) when given a choice of one among three art prints to view. Interest is important for choosing the object of attention, even if interest does not have a significant impact on deeply engaged reading. However, before any strong conclusion is made, additional research is needed to clarify the impact of interest on engaged reading.

Some Tentative Suggestions

1. Keep the workload (time and effort) low: even when there is a lack of interest, the chance of engaged reading is increased when visitors can process exhibit content quickly.
2. The value ratio (interest divided by cost) is a useful approach to understanding the interplay between interest and workload. The ratio of interest to workload is highly predictive of deeply engaged reading and should guide exhibit designers to consider the benefits and costs of design. Consider other aspects of design (in addition to number of words) that require more time and effort to process.

3. Measures of benefit other than interest may have a larger impact on visitor reading. For example, concreteness versus abstractness of exhibit content may contribute to both the ease of comprehension and enjoyment of viewing exhibits. After visitors are attracted by concrete objects, they may be more open to abstract ideas. In addition, a rating of expected satisfaction might be better than (or as good as) the interest rating used in these studies. Combining ratings of benefit with pre-knowledge and familiarity might also provide a more powerful predictor of reading than interest rating by itself.

The current studies are only a beginning in understanding how the value ratio and related measures influence engaged attention. It is my hope that these findings will stimulate additional research.

Table 8.1: Comparison of Parameters in the Three Studies

	Study 1	Study 2	Study 3
No. participants	43	40	20
No. art prints	20	25	20
Passage length, range (average no.)	49–315 (149.9)	49–230 (102.4)	62–230 (127.8)
Shorter range No. words (no. prints)	49–99 (7)	48–56 (5)	62–86 (5)
Medium range No. words (no. prints)	—	75–98 (10)	97–124 (5)
Longer range No. words (no. prints)	115–192 (4)	112–158 (7)	127–158 (7)
Longest passages No. words (no. prints)	204–315 (9)	> 200 (3)	> 200 (3)
Text layout	Paragraph	Bullets	Bullets
Reading measures	Read all	Average words read	Average words read
	Read some	Proportion read	Proportion read
	Read any	Recall	—

Table 8.2: Results for Each Artwork in Study 1

Artwork	Total Words	Interest Rating	Amount of Passage Read, % All	Some	Any	r-value
Degas-1	49	4.83	43.9	09.8	53.7	.099
Ernst	50	4.95	44.2	09.3	53.5	.099
Cot	72	5.78	32.6	37.2	69.8	.080
Hicks	74	5.68	37.2	34.9	72.1	.077
Picasso-1	88	4.50	25.6	34.9	72.1	.051
Seurat	91	4.53	11.6	34.9	46.5	.050
Wood	99	5.60	27.9	37.2	65.1	.057
		5.12	31.9	33.9	65.8	.073
Degas-2	115	5.65	24.4	43.9	68.3	.049
Gerome	120	6.25	14.0	41.9	55.9	.052
Miro-1	160	3.58	04.9	26.8	31.7	.022
Picasso-2	192	4.40	04.7	25.6	30.3	.023
		4.97	12.0	34.6	46.	.037
Picasso-3	204	5.05	0	48.8	48.2	.025
Renoir-1	216	4.62	04.8	45.2	50.0	.021
Monet	220	5.38	02.3	51.2	53.5	.017
Picasso-4	228	5.13	02.3	53.5	55.8	.023
Picasso-5	228	5.55	02.5	62.5	65.0	.024
Picasso-6	240	5.35	09.8	61.0	70.8	.022
Renoir-2	260	5.38	09.5	35.7	45.2	.021
Miro-2	276	3.75	02.4	40.5	42.9	.014
DaVinci	315	7.08	07.1	66.7	73.8	.023
		5.25	04.5	51.7	56.2	.021

Table 8.3: Results for Each Artwork in Study 2

Artist	Painting	Words	No. Bullets	Words Read	Proportion Read	Interest Rating	r-value
Mondrian	Landscape	49	2	39.2	80.0	4.33	.090
Van Gogh	Starry Night	54	3	47.5	87.9	5.67	.105
Mondrian	Landscape	65	3	51.2	78.8	5.73	.088
Morisot	Dining Rm	67	5	46.9	70.0	5.60	.084
Ingres	LeBlanc	56	3	39.5	70.5	4.96	.089
Mondrian	Horiz. Tree	75	3	43.5	57.7	4.69	.063
Seurat	Sunday PM	78	3	68.6	87.9	6.82	.089
Mondrian	Straight Lines	79	3	42.5	53.8	3.58	.045
DaVinci	Mona Lisa	77	4	63.4	82.3	7.91	.103
Picasso	Smoker	82	6	55.7	67.9	5.65	.069
Harnett	Old Violin	85	3	55.5	65.3	4.73	.056
Braque	Musical Form	91	4	49.7	54.6	4.69	.052
Gauguin	Maria	95	4	79.9	84.1	7.09	.057
Renoir	Mme Renoir	97	7	48.5	50.0	4.77	.049
Gainsborough	Countess	98	5	56.7	57.9	4.92	.050
Cot	Storm	112	5	74.1	66.2	6.27	.056
Whistler	Artist Mother	127	5	75.1	59.1	6.13	.048
Wood	Amer Gothic	136	6	83.6	61.5	6.20	.046
Manet	Boating	136	9	57.1	42.0	4.74	.022
Van Gogh	Starry Night	144	8	91.4	63.5	5.67	.039
DaVinci	Mona Lisa	147	8	86.9	59.1	5.80	.040
Gérôme	Pygmalion	158	10	85.6	54.2	6.69	.042
Gauguin	Maria	201	9	87.4	43.5	3.33	.017
El Greco	Toledo	215	10	83.4	38.8	6.19	.029
Seurat	Sunday PM	230	8	115.0	50.0	6.17	.027

Table 8.4: Results of Each Artwork in Study 3

Artist	Painting	No. Words	No. Bullets	Interest Rating	Mean Words Read	Proportion Read	r-value
Hicks	The Peaceable Kingdom	62	4	5.3	58.9	.95	.085
Modigliani	Italian Woman	67	4	3.8	49.0	.70	.057
Morisot	In the Dining Room	67	5	4.1	53.6	.80	.061
Picasso	The Smoker	82	6	5.2	50.8	.62	.063
Pollock	Autumn Rhythm	86	6	4.9	68.8	.80	.057
Renoir	Madame Renoir	97	7	4.2	37.8	.39	.043
Degas	Woman/ Chrysanth	102	5	5.0	73.4	.72	.049
Matisse	Lady in Blue	104	3	4.1	65.5	.63	.039
Manet	Olympia	104	4	4.4	65.5	.63	.042
Rousseau	Rain in the Jungle	124	7	5.9	75.6	.61	.048
Whistler	Arrangement. . . .	127	5	4.7	61.0	.48	.037
Wood	American Gothic	136	6	6.6	91.1	.67	.049
Manet	Boating	137	9	4.0	64.4	.47	.029
Van Gogh	Starry Night	144	8	8.0	106.6	.74	.056
DaVinci	Mona Lisa	147	8	7.6	101.4	.69	.052
Cezanne	Landscape with Viaduct	155	7	3.9	62.0	.40	.025
Gérôme	Pygmalion & Galatea	158	10	5.3	50.6	.32	.034
Gauguin	La Orano Maria	201	9	4.6	60.3	.30	.023
El Greco	View of Toledo	215	10	6.2	96.8	.45	.029
Seurat	Sunday Afternoon . . .	230	8	5.2	52.9	.23	.023

NOTE

The data from these three studies were originally part of the following conference presentations: Bitgood, Dukes, & Abby (2007); Bitgood, Dukes, & New (2006); Bitgood, New, & White (2008) "Projective focusing, engaged attention, and value: How do they relate to interest and reading?" Paper presented at the Annual Meeting of the Southern Society of Philosophy & Psychology, New Orleans, LA.

PART 3

Ways to Promote Engaged Attention

chapter 9

Prompting Engaged Attention with Visitor Self-Guides

▷ **KEY IDEAS** ◁

- Visitor attention can be increased in a number of ways, including prompting visitors to engage their attention to objects and interpretive devices.
- Methods of prompting engaged attention are described in this and the next several chapters (which make up Part 3).
- Self-guided devices can effectively prompt visitors to increase their engaged attention for the entire museum, for individual exhibitions within the museum, and/or for isolated exhibit objects.

Introduction

An online dictionary defines the verb "prompt" as "to hint, suggest, provoke, or induce" (Vocabulary Vocabulary 2007). "Prompting" is "something that gives incentive for action." The attention-value model provides a framework for prompting visitors to engage their attention more deeply in the content of museum exhibitions and programs. Prompting engaged attention can take many forms. This part of the book provides several examples of prompting visitor attention via (1) *self-guided devices* (this chapter), (2) *instructions to describe or compare objects* (Chapter 10), (3) *placing text next to the object it describes* (Chapter 11), *adding interpretive text to audio to give meaning to an exhibition gallery* (Chapter 12), and (4) *using life-sized animal cutouts* to prompt more engaged attention to zoo animals (Chapter 13).

A selective review of studies using self-guided devices to prompt increases in visitor attention is provided in this chapter. Self guides have taken several forms: museum guides, gallery/exhibition guides, worksheets for school groups, guides for individual exhibit objects, and, finally, guides for navigation

Attention and Value: Keys to Understanding Museum Visitors by Stephen Bitgood, 111–121.

(wayfinding). These self-guides can be used both for navigating through the museum and for inducing or provoking more deeply engaged attention to exhibits and programs.

Assessing the effectiveness of hand-carried self-guiding devices in museums should include three criteria: (1) *selection/distribution* (how often is the self-guide either taken by or given to the visitor?); (2) *usage* (degree to which and how visitors actually attempt to use the guide); and (3) *mental processing* (how effectively visitors process and act upon the information contained in the guide). Some of the studies in this chapter address the *selection* problem: what is the best way to encourage visitors to select the guide? How often do visitors take the guide if it is not handed to them? Other studies address the *usage* problem, although there is much that still needs to be accomplished for designing the most effective self-guides. Still other reports deal with the problem of influencing how information is *mentally processed* (e.g., "communicating empowering ideas"). Do visitors view more exhibit objects and learn more when they use the self-guides?

The following review is divided into five different types of guides: museum-wide guides, exhibition/gallery guides, school worksheets, guides for individual objects, and guides for navigation.

There is a dramatic increase in the museum use of electronic devices, including iPads, GPS devices, smartphones, etc. While there is no doubt that these devices are likely to eventually change the nature of visitor self-guiding, it is too early to know how these will be used most effectively. However, I believe they will serve the same functions as the handheld paper devices that have been used for years and that are reviewed in this chapter.

Museum Self-Guides

Museums often use self-guides for the entire museum that are either handed to visitors as they enter or are available for visitors to pick up on their own. The facilities using these self-guides include all types of museums, zoos, and parks. Self-guides often combine functions (e.g., used both as interpretive supplements and navigation aids). Self-guides are also sometimes used to offer guidance to visitors in their own language without having to design text labels in multiple languages. Five examples of self-guidance assessments are briefly described. The examples include a wide range of exhibition centers: an art museum, a natural history museum, a science center, a botanical garden, and the National Park Service.

Robinson (1928) examined pamphlet usage in art museums (see Chapter 2). Although his first attempt was disappointing because visitors could not find the paintings described in the pamphlet, his second study (after improving the device) was more successful. (This may have been the first formative evaluation conducted in a museum.) He found that his final pamphlet produced the following results: (1) the average time of the total visit was increased from 17 to 28 minutes; (2) the average number of paintings observed increased from 30 to 46 minutes; and (3) the average time per picture during the last part of the visit (when visitors are usually satiated and spend less time per picture) was increased.

Porter (1938) compared the effects of two types of guides with a no-guide condition. One type of guide was designed to emphasize the planned sequence of exhibits to demonstrate the story of organic evolution. The other type was nonsequenced, merely giving information without relating it to the story of evolution. With no guide, visitors averaged 21.4 minutes on the first floor of the Peabody Museum. With the sequenced guide, visitors averaged 32.5 minutes; with the nonsequenced guide, visitors averaged 37.9 minutes. There was no statistically significant difference between the two guides, but either guide produced significantly longer visitation than no guide. Guided visitors engaged in more label reading than unguided visitors, although this difference tended to decrease with time in the museum. Guided visitors also examined more cases (both those mentioned and not mentioned in the guide) than unguided visitors. Unfortunately, knowledge gain was not measured: it might have revealed a difference between sequenced and nonsequenced guides.

Borun (1977) studied three different types of visitor guides in the Franklin Institute of Science. The first guide (*Highlights Tour*) recommended a sequence of exhibits, floor by floor. The second type (*Search & Discover*) was designed as a game for younger children. It consisted of questions that required children to look carefully at exhibits. The third guide (*Museum Adventure Trail*) was designed for older children. It consisted of 15 questions that could be found in various exhibit areas. The *Highlights* group did not show any positive changes in learning, in attitudes toward science, or feelings about the museum. The *Search & Discover* game and the Museum *Adventure Trail* guide, on the other hand, both showed positive changes in all three areas (learning, attitudes toward science, and feelings about the museum). Consistent with the attention-value model, the guides offering higher value (e.g., game and question versions) would be expected to provide higher motivation because of higher value ratios. The game and questions are likely to increase satisfaction, the numerator of the value ratio.

Korn (1988) assessed the effects of two types of self-guiding brochures at the Chicago Botanic Garden. The only difference between the guides was the use of declarative statement headings versus inquisitive (question) headings. Visitors without guides scored lower on the measure of learning (multiple-choice test) than either guide group, but there was no statistical difference between the two groups receiving the guides.

While not equivalent to museums, national parks are comparable to museums in many ways. Self-guided devices are apparently popular in the national parks. The National Park Service (2003) reported that 62 percent of park users indicated they used the park brochure and 33 percent used the self-guided tour. The self-guided tour was rated highest as the "most important interpretive media type," and the park brochure was rated almost as high. Ranger-aided programs were third in importance rating.

The studies using facility-wide self-guides demonstrate that these devices often increase viewing time and learning. In addition, visitors consider them to be an important interpretive media. However, the studies reviewed here do not tell us what makes them successful. The attention-value model argues that most of the same characteristics that make exhibit labels successful will also contribute to the effectiveness of self-guides.

Exhibition Self-Guides

Guides for specific exhibitions are probably used at least as commonly as guides to the whole museum. These guides can take several forms (e.g., inexpensive or expensive paper, recyclable laminated device), with each form likely to have its own advantages and disadvantages.

Birney (1990) reported an evaluation of recyclable laminated guides in the *Tropic World* exhibition of the Brookfield Zoo. Visitors who used the guides stayed longer than nonguided visitors. Observational scanning found that the guides were widely used and increased visitors' abilities to locate and identify animals in the exhibits. Only a small percentage of laminated guides were not returned as visitors exited the building.

Don Patterson and I compared visitors who used one-page exhibition guides with those who used no guides (Bitgood & Patterson, 1987). Visitors to the *Alabama Cave* exhibition at the Anniston Museum of Natural History and to the *Predator* building of the Birmingham Zoo were given handouts with ten questions each. The answers to the handouts were contained in the exhibit labels. The study addressed several questions:

1. Is it possible to increase reading by using a handout that prompts visitors to read?
2. What is the best method of getting visitors to use the handout device?
3. If the handout does increase visitor attention, how long will it last during the course of viewing an exhibition?
4. Will different measures of attention (stopping to read, time spent reading, and total viewing time) be correlated with one another?

The two studies found: (1) the best way to ensure visitors receive a handout was by handing it to visitors; (2) visitors using the handout were much more likely to read label text than those who did not have the handout; (3) average reading time more than doubled during the first six exhibits for the handout condition compared to the no-handout condition: after that, there was little difference between the two condition; and (4) total viewing time was consistency greater for the handout condition, but decreased across exhibits viewed.

DeWaard, Jagmin, Maistro, & McNamara (1974) compared four groups: (1) cards with questions about the exhibit; (2) cards with questions and supplementary information; (3) cards with questions plus feedback; and (4) a control group without cards. Groups with cards performed better than those without cards, but there was no significant difference among the groups using cards. As with many of these studies, any well-designed handout seems to have a positive impact on directing visitor attention.

Loomis (1982) evaluated a self-guide for the *Maya* traveling exhibition at the Denver Art Museum. The guide described six objects with illustrated drawings. The self-guide was considered helpful, it made the objects more interesting, and it told visitors things they did not know. Also, visitors wanted self-guides available at selected exhibits. Less than one-half indicated that it was easy to read and use and that it should be made available for free. Most respondents agreed that the guides could be used as a source of more detailed information, as a self-guide, as a bibliographical source, and as a keepsake/memento. Fewer visitors thought it was useful as something to pass on to family or friends and/or as a set of guides to collect. When guides were not handed to visitors, only 4 percent of visitors actually picked up the guide and 2 percent entered the room with the guide. The distribution box did not attract visitor attention. Recommendations for self-guide use included: (1) developing an effective distribution system (e.g., guards might suggest that people use guides); (2) designing guides so they help visitors locate objects (observing traffic flow patterns before designing guides should help with the effectiveness of orientation); (3) supplementing rather than duplicating other interpretation; (4) and making the guide brief, keeping in mind that visitors are walking around and looking at objects. Loomis argued that guides could serve a variety of purposes: source of supplemental information, keepsake, bibliographic source, self-guide, something to pass on to family/friends, and as a set to collect. He also suggested that guides be offered in alternative languages.

In a detailed experimental study, Screven (1975) compared several forms of guidance devices on visitors to the Renwick Gallery (part of the Smithsonian

Institution). The following hand-carried devices were used: (1) a punchboard (responder punched a hole in a card and was given feedback for correct answers in the form of a green light); (2) an audiotape; and (3) a flip booklet (70 cards bound together on a spiral binder). A number of groups were studied, including several control groups (e.g., no handheld guidance devices and flip booklet without seeing the exhibit). Visitor learning was most effective with the flip booklet and audiotapes. However, more visitors quit without finishing the program when using the flip booklet and self-paced audiotape than with a tape-paced audiotape. The self-paced audiotape used an automatic-stop function when questions were asked, whereas the tape-paced audio did not stop automatically. The audiotape was also rated higher than the flip booklet.

LeClaire and Grabski (2010) studied the use of gallery guides in the *Tete-a-Tete* exhibition at the Frye Art Museum in Seattle. The exhibition displayed 150 artworks in a salon-style arrangement. The guide was a laminated four-page map of the gallery and contained minimal information: titles, artists, and dates of paintings. Compared with non-guide users, gallery-guide users spent more time in the exhibition and recalled information more readily. Enjoyment ratings of the viewing experience were not significantly different from those who did not use the guide. One can only speculate whether more detailed information on the guide (rather than just titles, artists, and dates) would have produced higher satisfaction.

In summary, these studies of exhibition guides provide more information (than the museum guide studies) about what makes them work. The problem of distribution (letting visitors pick them up versus handing them to visitors) is an important consideration. Keeping information on the guide to a minimum and easy to access seems to increase usage. However, how much is too much is not clear. Overall, the studies strongly suggest that when the self-guides are used, they increase engagement with exhibits and learning.

School Worksheets

Teachers often give worksheet assignments to students with instructions to complete during the museum field trip. The worksheet device is a way to prompt students to focus their attention more deeply on relevant educational content of the museums. One of the differences between worksheets and other types of guides is that there are usually consequences from the teacher if they are not correctly completed. At least two evaluators have studied worksheet usage.

Fry (1987) examined the use of school worksheets. While this study deals with the use of worksheets with school groups, much of the discussion is applicable to the use of museum guides. The content and style of the guide are undoubtedly important. Fry suggested several guidelines for worksheets: (1) they should emphasize teaching concepts rather than facts; (2) they should relate information to prior knowledge; (3) they need to be checked for ambiguity of meaning; and (4) they should be designed so that they are easily used.

McManus (1985) compared the impact of worksheets on younger (under 10 years old) and older (10 to 16 years old) groups of children during a visit at the British Museum (Natural History). The worksheet condition was compared with groups who did not have worksheets. Audio recordings of conversations were taped during the visit. There was a difference between the younger and older groups and between worksheet and nonworksheet groups in terms of "worksheet management problems" and attention to exhibits. Adults with younger children tended to complete the sheet for the younger child. The worksheet did help focus attention on items from the worksheet, but after the worksheet was completed, the younger children focused on other aspects of the exhibits. Younger children with the worksheet viewed exhibits longer (186 seconds) compared with those without the worksheet (41 seconds). Management problems (e.g., finding places to write) took up much of the additional viewing time. Older children usually worked without supervision and demonstrated less involvement with exhibits than younger children. The parents of younger children tended to assist and help direct the children. Older children working by themselves acted like the worksheets were a chore (less fun).

Individual or Pairs of Exhibit Objects

While museum and gallery/exhibition guides are used often, guides for individual exhibit objects are used less often. The examples in this section describe innovative projects from the Denver Museum of Art.

Chambers (1990) examined the impact of an interpretive device on a single art object at the Denver Museum of Art. The goal of this study was to design a label for the Toledo installation of a David Hockney photo-collage exhibition that would not just provide specific information, but communicate "empowering ideas." An "empowering idea" included the following criteria: (1) help the visitor understand an exhibition; (2) enable the visitor to expound on what is presented by adding his/her own experience to give it meaning; (3) may be applied to other art exhibitions; and (4) may stimulate the visitor to inquire about other aspects of life. The device consisted of a structure that held three pockets each with a paddle containing interpretation. The paddles had titles such as "What the Artist Chose to Show," "What You Chose to See," and "What the Object Has to Say." These headings give factual information while provoking the visitors to relate the information to their own unique experiences. The intention is to make the experience of the novice somewhat comparable to the expert's.

Chambers and Muir (1990) provided another study from the Denver Museum of Art focused on individual artworks; however, this time visitors were prompted to compare two different paintings. Novice viewers tend to view art in a more emotional way and consider what is pleasing to the eye rather than using the aesthetic principles of an "expert." The brochure was designed to help guide the novice art viewer to have an aesthetic experience with an art object by teaching skills of aesthetic observation.

Bouguereau's painting *Two Girls* was used in the project because it has a strong emotional appeal. The label addressed the role of emotions in forming value or critical judgments about artwork. A brochure was designed to compare the *Two Girls* painting to Degas' *Woman Scratching Her Back*, an artwork that does not have pleasant appeal to most viewers. The goal was to enable the viewer to look at the Degas painting from a different perspective, facilitating a critical judgment without relying strictly on emotional appeal. The brochure was intended to be intellectually stimulating without becoming too detailed for the novice viewer. The mock-up brochure used for testing included black and white reproductions of each of the works (allowing the visitor to locate the works quickly). It also contained a quote from each artist to familiarize the viewer with the attitudes that influenced these works.

The first section of the brochure walked the visitor through the paintings and was popular with visitors. However, the second section, describing theory and content, was confusing to many visitors. The title of the second section was changed and the wording revised. The brochures appeared to help visitors gain confidence in their ability to approach art with a more informed attitude.

A third study at the Denver Museum of Art also attempted to prompt visitors to examine art using the tools of an expert. Krulick and Ritchie (1990) used the interpretive "paddle" device similar to that in Chamber's study. The novice's experience is based largely on emotion while the expert's experience involves several other factors such as perception, emotion, communication, and intellect. The primary goals of the project were to teach skills, awareness, and ideas that would broaden the novice's experience and enable the visitor to use those skills with other art objects. Thomas Cole's painting *Dream of Arcadia* was chosen for the project because of its popularity. To invite visitors to spend time with this artwork, the staff created an inviting atmosphere by placing comfortable chairs to sit in, fresh-cut flowers, and a rug. Pull-out paddles with interpretive information were placed on the wall near the painting. The visitor could pull out one or more paddles to learn about the painting. Each paddle corresponded to the four factors (perception, emotion, communication, intellect) that appear to influence the expert's experience. The paddles introduced ways to understand and better enjoy the painting and used quotes from Cole to help visitors feel as though they were getting acquainted with the artist. Most of the visitors (82 percent) used the exhibition area and label. About 40 percent used the seating, and of those who were seated, 90 percent looked at the painting while sitting. The average time spent looking at the painting was 1 minute, 8 seconds, and the average total time spent in the area was 2 minutes, 32 seconds. (Prior to the project, 47.3 percent of visitors looked at the painting, and the average looking time was 27 seconds; only 67 percent of those people used the seating.) Most people (68 percent) removed one paddle, and 23 percent removed all four. Most of the visitors (88 percent) said the labels enabled them to see things they would not have seen otherwise, and 86 percent said they learned skills that they could apply to other experiences with art (spending time with an exhibit, looking for details, etc.).

Navigation Self-Guides

Howes (1990) examined the effectiveness of newly designed handheld maps. The study involved several steps. First, visitors were observed and interviewed. Those who seemed to have trouble finding their way were identified and interviewed. Next, problems were identified from the observations and interviews. Finally, from the information gathered, three target areas were identified: architecture, signage, and maps.

The building's architecture served as an impediment to the visitors' museum experience since it prevented free circulation flow and made it difficult to locate services such as restrooms and food service. Two architectural characteristics were particularly problematic. The first was that the three floor levels are not continuous between one part of the museum and another. Visitors had to change floors to view all of the twentieth-century collections. The second architectural problem was that the first and second floors often required visitors to change floors without knowing they had done so.

Signage was the next problematic area. The use of signs is extremely limited in the museum. The size, legibility, color, lighting, language, and symbols used in signage were examined carefully. In addition, signage terms were made consistent so that the signs would be more effective. Direction sign location was also considered carefully.

The last area of concern was navigation. Wayfinding maps were revised to include changes such as the location of the restrooms, the addition of primary street names and dates in the galleries to indicate sequence and chronology, and the alteration of confusing names on maps to avoid visitor confusion.

After these changes were made, guards reported fewer questions about locating galleries. Wayfinding was apparently improved.

Carey Tisdal and I (Bitgood & Tisdal, 1996) examined the impact of lobby orientation on visitors at the St. Louis Science Center. One aspect of this study compared two groups of visitors: those who received the visitor guide as they entered the Center lobby and those who did not have a visitor guide. The use of the visitor guide appeared to be critical to first-time visitors. First time visitors were more likely than repeaters to use the guide. First-timers who used the visitor guide gave an average rating of visitor satisfaction on a 10-point scale compared with those who did not use the guide. There was little difference in satisfaction, however, between repeat visitors who used the guide and repeaters who did not. First-time visitors who used the guide stayed in the museum three times longer than those who did not use the guide. Repeat visitors who used the guide averaged slightly shorter times than those who did not use the guide. Omnimax moviegoers who used the guide had an average total museum time of 5.4 hours compared with 2.9 hours for non-guide users who attended the movie.

Conclusion

Self-guided devices are a cost-effective way to engage visitor attention. The studies reported in this chapter indicate that:

1. Self-guides come in a variety of forms (e.g., paper, laminated sheets, hand-carried paddles). The physical characteristics of the device may be less important than the content, organization, and how it is distributed.
2. Total time in the museum (or exhibition) can be significantly increased with the use of guides. The number of text labels people read can also be increased with self-guides as prompts.
3. Learning (when it has been measured) increases with the use of self-guided devices.
4. Other positive outcomes may also occur (e.g., change in attitudes and perception of the museum).

While additional research can identify the most important variables for cost-effective, self-guided devices, there is no doubt that prompting engaged attention with self-guided devices is an important tool for museums to increase deeply engaged attention to exhibits and programs.

Self guides, similar to other types of prompting approaches, have several advantages: (1) they are more cost-effective than making expensive changes in the exhibition itself; (2) they can target specific types of outcomes and audiences; (3) they usually approach the problem of visitor attention directly (e.g., tell visitors where to look, what to do) rather than through subtle design; and (4) the resulting visitor attention often generalizes to other aspects of visitor attention. Successful guides are likely to have an effective distribution system, be easy to use (low cost), and provide high satisfaction (have high interest, provoke curiosity, etc.).

NOTE

The material in this chapter is based, to some extent, on material from Bitgood and Davis (1992).

chapter 10

Prompting Engaged Attention by Instructions to Describe or Compare Exhibit Objects

▷ **KEY IDEAS** ◁

- Prompting visitor attention can lead to both an immediate response (e.g., verbally describing an exhibit object) and a subsequent response (e.g., reading text material about the object described).
- Prompting engaged attention can be accomplished in many ways, including by simple instructions, by suggesting a reaction or activity (e.g., "Look for the hidden animal") or by providing a provocative statement or question ("Which plant is a cactus?").
- In two separate studies, individuals were prompted to describe or compare artworks, asked to rate interest in seeing information about the art, and finally given a chance to read from a text passage related to the artwork.
- Prompting engagement (describing or comparing artwork) had a large impact on reading text passages, and a smaller impact on interest rating.
- Study 2 also demonstrated the importance of having a choice among alternative objects.

Introduction

From the museum perspective, the mental processing that accompanies engaged attention has three important characteristics:

1. **Processing level.** Shallow processing requires little effort and could be described as more "mindless" in that the resources of attention go unchallenged. Recognition of a familiar object without much consideration of its meaning involves shallow processing. Reading a difficult text passage, on the other hand, requires considerable mental effort and involves

Attention and Value: Keys to Understanding Museum Visitors by Stephen Bitgood, 122–131.

deeper processing. In general, the more abstract the thinking, the deeper the processing required.

2. **Activity duration.** Deeper mental processing is likely to take longer than shallow processing. Duration can be called "persistence" and is often associated with engaged attention generalizing to a new activity. If visitors are prompted to verbally describe an exhibit object, they are also more likely to read more text about the object than if they had not been prompted to describe the object.

3. **Content focus.** The inferred outcome (e.g., learning, inquiry, immersion, flow) is obviously related to the specific content to which visitors are exposed. For example, if the physical characteristics overwhelm the abstract meaning (as in a European museum I visited with a beautiful, 30-foot model of DNA), the size and aesthetic characteristics may be the focus of engagement to the detriment of understanding the biological importance of the double helix.

More than a decade ago, my colleagues and I (Bitgood, Devia, Goodwin, et al., 2001) used a technique we called "projective focusing" designed to focus attention on artworks. In the study, participants were asked to verbally describe what "comes to mind" when viewing each print. Worts (1989) used a similar method (which he termed "reflective imaging") in a guided imagery activity in which an audio track encouraged participants to engage in immersive imagery associated with a work of art. Instead of "projective focusing" I am now calling this method "prompted engagement" because it appears to facilitate mindful or engaged attention. One additional example: in one of my studies (Bitgood, 2011c) I found that visitors are more likely to experience a feeling of immersion if they are encouraged by a text prompting them to imagine themselves in a particular time and place.

"Prompted engagement" can be defined as an activity that occurs to a prompt and that facilitates deep mental processing of sensory, perceptual, and/or cognitive information. In terms of the attention-value model, prompted engagement is a way to encourage people to process exhibit content more deeply, making it more likely to produce desirable outcomes such as learning. Prompting activities might include a variety of techniques, such as imagery exercises (e.g., Worts, 1993), description ("Describe this artwork"), comparative analysis ("Compare and contrast these two artworks"), free association ("What comes to mind when you look at this artwork?"), or storyline prompting ("Tell me a story about this artwork").

Study 1

The first study in this chapter compares two prompting conditions (descriptive and comparative) with a control condition. The descriptive method asked participants to describe each art print. In the comparative condition, participants were instructed to compare two art prints on several characteristics. Following the prompting engagement activity, participants rated their interest in seeing information about the art print; then, they were given the opportunity to read all, some, or none of a text passage. Individuals in the control condition were instructed to view the artwork as long as they desired, but they were not instructed to engage in any active, overt processing before rating the interest level for the art prints and then choosing how much of the text passages to read. From previous studies (see Chapter 8), we know that increased reading of passages occurs when the costs are decreased (i.e., the number of words in the passage are reduced). In this study, we attempted to determine whether reading can be influenced by prompting deeply engaged attention to the artwork.

Prompted engagement (describing or comparing artworks) is expected to increase reading of text material associated with the artwork. However, it is not clear what impact prompted engagement might have on interest rating. If interest rating represents a stable disposition (individual interest), no immediate change in interest is likely to occur. If, on the other hand, interest is easily influenced by the context (situational interest), then interest rating would be increased as a result of prompted engagement.

Method

PARTICIPANTS. Thirty-eight undergraduate students recruited from introductory psychology at Jacksonville State University served as participants. Students received extra credit for their participation. The study was conducted during the fall of 2008.

MATERIALS. Twenty art prints from the Metropolitan Museum of Art's *Metropolitan Seminars in Art* series (Canaday 1958) were used in this study. In addition, text passages of varying length (56 to 230 words) were provided for each print. Passages were divided into bulleted statements (ranging from two to ten). (See Appendix B for examples of the text passages.)

PROCEDURES AND EXPERIMENTAL DESIGN. The purpose of the study was described to each participant, who was seated on the opposite side of a table from the experimenter. Participants were randomly divided into three conditions:

1. **Descriptive prompting.** Participants were instructed to examine the art print(s) carefully and describe what they see.

2. **Comparative prompting.** Participants were instructed to examine two prints presented simultaneously and compare the prints on specific characteristics.
3. **Control.** Participants passively viewed the art prints; no prompting activity was used for this group.

Following the prompting activity (or passive viewing), participants were asked to give a rating from 1 (lowest) to 10 (highest) on how interested they would be to see information about the artwork. Once they gave an interest rating, the art print was turned over and a passage of text of varying length was revealed. Participants had the choice of reading (out loud) none, some, or all of the text. The experimenter checked off each bullet as it was read so that the proportion of the passage could be computed.

To summarize, the response-impact (dependent) measures were interest rating and proportion of text passage read, and the person-setting (independent) variable was prompted engagement.

Results and Discussion

PROMPTING ENGAGED READING. The two prompting techniques were both associated with a higher proportion of text reading than the control condition (see Table 10.1). This table shows that the average percentage of passage read was 55.5 percent for descriptive focusing, 62.4 percent for comparative focusing, and 48.5 percent for the control condition. Analysis of variance

Table 10.1: Impact of Prompting Conditions on Reading and Interest

Mean Proportion of the Text Passage Read

Condition	N	Mean Proportion Read
Descriptive	12	.555
Comparative	14	.624
Control	12	.485

Rating of Interest

Condition	N	Interest Rating (on scale of 1 to 10)
Descriptive	12	5.02
Comparative	14	5.52
Control	12	4.96

(ANOVA) revealed a significant difference between the prompting and control conditions, but not between the types of prompting.

IMPACT OF PROMPTING ON INTEREST RATING. Despite its impact on reading (as Table 10.1 shows), prompted engagement had a statistically insignificant impact on interest rating although the comparative condition resulted in higher ratings (5.52 on a scale of 1 to 10) than the descriptive (5.02) or control (4.96) groups. If interest is a stable construct, it makes sense that it would not be easily changed by a single manipulation.

This study demonstrates that prompting effort (describing or comparing artwork) can result in an increase in subsequent persistent reading. There was also a smaller difference in interest rating between the comparative versus other two conditions.

The fact that the interest rating was not significantly influenced by prompted engagement could be the result of a relatively small sample for each condition or it could reflect the stability of interest rating. Since the proportion of the text passage read was significantly affected by prompted engagement, the latter explanation (stability of interest) may be at least partially accurate.

Study 2

Study 1 shows that prompted engagement (instructions to describe or compare artworks) influences reading. Prompted engagement may have also influenced interest rating, but the effect was not statistically significant. Study 2 examines two aspects of the visitor attention-value theory. First, as a follow up to Study 1, the effect of prompting individuals to describe artwork on interest rating and reading is examined. Second, the study assessed how choice influences engaged attention. Combining prompting and choice provided a window into the interaction between choice and prompting.

The prompting procedures used in this study were similar to those used in Study 1 with one exception. Instead of two prompting methods (describing and comparing), only describing was used in the current study.

As implied by the term "free-choice learning," choice is a major consideration when visiting a museum. Visitors choose what to do, where to go, and what to attend to. While choice is an obviously critical factor, few visitor researchers have given it adequate consideration other than to report on the percentage of visitors who stop (usually called "attracting power") at specific exhibits. For whatever reason, visitors are selective: they choose to stop at some exhibit elements and not others. What are the factors that influence this choice? Rounds (2004) relates the curiosity-driven museum visitor's decision-making to optimal foraging theory, suggesting decision-making rules for searching, handling, and quitting that might explain how visitors select exhibit elements to which to attend. As far as I know, Rounds's model has not been tested in any empirical studies (see Chapter 4).

One of the important characteristics of visitor choice occurs when visitors are offered an increasing number of objects from which to choose. Along with two of my colleagues, I (Bitgood, McKerchar, & Dukes, 2012) suggested that studies by Melton (1935) and Porter (1938) demonstrate that as the number of objects to view increases, visitors are likely to become more selective (i.e., they choose a smaller proportion of available objects). The database collected by Serrell (1998) reveals a similar pattern when comparing the percentage of stopping for exhibitions with the fewest number of components with those with the largest number. The greater the number of exhibit elements, the smaller the proportion of stops.

Study Rationale

Study 2 examined (1) the impact of prompted engagement on interest and reading; (2) the influence of choice on viewing time, interest, and reading; and (3) the interaction between prompting and choice.

Method

PARTICIPANTS. Sixty participants were recruited from undergraduate psychology classes at Jacksonville State University during the spring semester of 2009. Students ranging in age from 18 to 39 years were given extra credit for their participation. Students reported little or no experience in art museums.

MATERIALS AND APPARATUS. Forty-five prints measuring 8.5 x 11 inches from artworks of well-known artists were used. These prints were taken from the Metropolitan Seminars in Art series by John Canaday (1958). The art prints ranged in content across many periods of art (see Tables 8.2, 8.3, and 8.4 for examples). A plastic sleeve protected each print. On the reverse side of the print was placed a text passage of varying length from 58 to 229 words. The passage was divided into bulleted sections that varied from three to ten bullets per art print and about 20 to 30 words per bullet.

A wooden panel that held up to three prints was used as a print holder. It contained a lip on the bottom to support the prints. The panel was 12 inches high and 36 inches wide and sat at an angle for easy viewing.

Data sheets consisted of a replica of each text passage in the order of presentation. They were divided into seven different sequences. The data sheets allowed for an accurate recording of each bullet read (word for word), the time spent describing, and an interest rating for each art print.

GENERAL PROCEDURE. The participant was seated at a table across from two experimenters. One of the experimenters read the instructions throughout the session while the other collected the data. The sessions were audio taped with permission from the participant. The tapes were used to obtain reliability checks after the session was completed and to rate the reading fluency of each participant, since reading ability is likely to influence the level of effort required to read the passages.

EXPERIMENTAL CONDITIONS.

Prompted engagement. Similar to Study 1, some participants were instructed to verbally describe the art print (active viewing) and others were instructed to look at the print as long as they wished (passive viewing).

Choice versus no choice. One half of the trial involved choice and the other half involved no choice. For the no-choice condition, three art prints were placed on the print holder in front of the participant and three separate trials were conducted. A trial consisted of selecting the print farthest to the left and following the procedure outlined below. The next and last trial consisted of selecting the middle print and finally the last print and following the same procedures. For the choice condition, three art prints were placed on the print holder in front of the participant. Only one trial was completed in this condition: the participant was asked to choose one favorite among the three prints presented and follow the procedures described below.

TRIAL PROCEDURES. The following procedures were used for the *active viewing* participants. The only difference between the conditions was that in the *choice* condition, participants were asked to pick up and describe one art print; in the *no choice* condition, participants were instructed to pick up and describe all three prints individually, from left to right. They did not have a choice in this condition. The three prints were placed on the wooden print holder in front of the participant, who was instructed to look at the prints and select one by picking it up; then, participants were asked to describe the painting and to say whatever comes to mind. When finished describing, the participants were instructed to return the print back to the holder. The second experimenter recorded the total time from when the print was picked up to when it was replaced. Next, a rating of interest was obtained by asking the participant to "rate the painting on a scale with 1 being the lowest and 10 being the highest, indicating how interested you would be in seeing information about the artwork and artist." After the participant's interest rating was recorded, the art print was turned over by the experimenter to reveal the text passage. Participants were asked to read (out loud) as much or as little of the text as they wished. They could read none of the passage, some of the passage, or all of the passage. The second experimenter then recorded the total number of bullets read. In previous studies, we found that once subjects began reading a bulleted statement, they almost always read the complete statement. However, if the participant stopped in the middle of a bulleted statement, the words read in that bullet were circled on the data sheet.

In the *passive viewing* condition, the same procedures were used with one exception: the participants were only asked to *examine or view* the art prints rather than provide a verbal description.

Seven sequences of trials were used in the study. The order in which each participant received the sequences was altered to control for any order effects. The number of bullets per condition was controlled so that they received an average of six bullets per art print. For each condition, the total number of bullets for the three prints being presented was the same.

After completing all of the sequences, a postexperiment survey was administered to the participants to obtain information about demographics, interest in art, frequency of museum visits, and ratings about fatigue, satiation, and perceived workload on a rating scale of 1 to 10 (1 being the lowest and 10 being the highest).

Results and Discussion

The choice variable was assessed by a within-subject comparison: some trials allowed a choice of which art print to view and other trials did not. Prompted engagement, on the other hand, was evaluated by a between-group comparison: one group (active viewing) was instructed to verbally describe the artwork, while the other group (passive viewing) simply viewed the artwork without comment.

THE IMPACT OF CHOICE: PROMPTED ENGAGEMENT. Table 10.2 summarizes the findings for viewing time, interest rating, and percentage of the passage read. The data are divided into prompting conditions (prompted engagement and passive viewing) and choice conditions (choice and no choice). (The statistical analysis [ANOVA] is available from the author upon request.)

VIEWING TIME. As expected, prompting engagement resulted in significantly longer viewing times than passive viewing. Choice also resulted in significantly longer viewing times than no choice. Given the prompt to describe the artwork, this outcome is not surprising. It was also expected that, when given a choice, viewing time would be longer than when no choice was given.

INTEREST RATING. Prompting resulted in a significant difference in ratings in that those in the passive viewing condition gave higher interest ratings (6.4) than those in the prompted engagement condition (5.4). In this case, engaged

Table 10.2: Comparison of Prompted Engagement and Choice

Viewing Time, seconds	Choice	No Choice
Prompted engagement	29.8	25.4
Passive view	13.7	9.4

Interest Rating, 1 to 10	Choice	No Choice
Prompted engagement	6.2	4.6
Passive view	7.1	5.7

Percentage Read	Choice	No Choice
Prompted engagement	60.7	56.3
Passive view	60.0	39.8

Data from Bitgood, New, & White (2008).

attention appeared to decrease interest rating, perhaps because some of the curiosity associated with the artwork is reduced as a result of examining it carefully.

The choice condition resulted in significantly higher average interest rating (6.7) than for the no choice condition (5.2). This makes sense because the higher-interest artworks are most likely to be selected when given a choice.

PERCENTAGE READING. In the choice condition, reading occurred at about the same level for prompted engagement (60.7 percent) as for passive viewing (60.0 percent). However, in the no-choice condition, reading levels for the passive viewing condition were markedly lower (39.8 percent) compared with the prompted engagement condition (56.3 percent). Choice may neutralize the impact of prompted engagement on reading.

General Discussion

The findings from the two studies in this chapter lead to the following conclusions:

1. The results of Study 1 were at least partially replicated: prompted engagement is an effective method of increasing reading (engaged attention) at least when no choice is available.
2. Choice appears to be an even more powerful variable than prompted engagement.

3. By its very nature, choice influences interest level, since people tend to choose objects to view that have a higher interest level.

Being able to choose high-interest objects to view and to ignore others suggests the selective nature of visitor attention in museums. There is evidence consistent with the notion that as the number of alternative choices increases, visitors become more selective and view a smaller proportion of objects available. Two studies reviewed in Chapter 2 are examples of selective choice. The first is Melton's (1935) study, in which number of paintings in a gallery increased and the percentage of stopping decreased. The other study is by Porter (1938), whose findings are also consistent with increased selectiveness since the percentage of stopping was correlated with number of exhibit cases in each gallery. In addition, Serrell's (1998) database of studies provides additional support for increased selectiveness. The exhibitions with the fewest number of elements had a significantly higher percentage of stopping (attracting power) than the exhibitions with the largest number of elements.

chapter 11

How Label Placement Influences Visitor Attention

▷ **KEY IDEAS** ◁

- The attention-value model suggests that placement of labels is important for two reasons: (1) detection (easier to see the label); and (2) cost (time and effort) is lower.
- Three studies in this chapter provide evidence that reading is more likely when the exhibit label is placed on the railing close to the object that it describes and where visitors usually stop to view the object.

Introduction

How often have you observed artwork placed in the middle of a gallery with no interpretation on or near it? If you are a savvy art museum visitor, you start searching all the walls to determine where the label might be. The physical proximity of interpretive labels to exhibit objects is critical. According to the attention-value model, the relationship between the label and the object it describes is important for two reasons: (1) *attention capture* (labels close to the objects are more likely to be noticed); and (2) the *value* of engaged reading (reading requires less effort if the label is close to the object it describes). This chapter reports data from three visitor institutions: two zoos and a natural history museum. The findings are consistent: label placement on the railing (line-of-sight placement) is the most effective location for getting visitors to pay attention.

The major purpose of exhibit labels in museums, parks, and zoos is to interpret exhibit content to the visiting public. Toward this end there has been considerable effort to develop labels that communicate their message effectively (see Bitgood, 2000; Rand, 1985; Screven, 1986; Serrell, 1983, 1996; and Shettel, et al., 1968). Museum professionals often lament, however, that visitors rarely take time to read the labels despite the time and effort it takes

---

Attention and Value: Keys to Understanding Museum Visitors by Stephen Bitgood, 132–136.

to develop attractive labels that are capable of communicating their message effectively. The major thesis of this chapter is that effective labels require more than a clear message written in a digestible form on an attractive surface. The placement of exhibit labels also plays a critical role in the communication process between the exhibition design team and visitors. The location of a label (as well as text content and physical features such as label length and text size) has considerable impact on its effectiveness.

Three studies carried out on different exhibitions and at different facilities are summarized in this chapter. These studies assessed the effects of label placement on visitor attention.

Method

Anniston Museum of Natural History

The first study was correlational in nature; it was conducted during the fall of 1988 and the spring of 1989 in the Attack & Defense Gallery of the Anniston Museum of Natural History; a more detailed account of the data can be found in Bitgood, Conroy, Pierce, Patterson, and Boyd (1989). Visitors were unobtrusively tracked through the exhibit gallery and their behavior at each exhibit carefully recorded. Behaviors of interest included where visitors stopped and what objects and labels they appeared to be viewing. Label reading (attending to a label for more than five seconds) was later correlated with position of the labels. Positions of interest included: high vertical placement (seven or more feet off the floor); line-of-sight placement (placed so that labels could be easily observed as visitors moved through the exhibit), and rear placement (placed so that visitors had to turn away from viewing the exhibit object/animals to read them). Data were collected by Jacksonville State University students, and occasional interobserver reliability checks were made between observers to ensure consistent measurement.

Birmingham Zoo

The second study was completed on a single weekend day in the summer of 1989 in the newly opened Social Animal Building of the Birmingham (Alabama) Zoo. This study was also correlational in nature. As in the first study, visitors were unobtrusively tracked through the exhibition area and their attention to exhibit labels carefully recorded. Graduate and advanced undergraduate students from Jacksonville State University served as data collectors under the close supervision of two of the authors. The percentage of visitors who attended to each label for more than five seconds was later correlated with the position of the label.

North Carolina Zoo

The third study was carried out in the summer and fall of 1989 at several exhibit areas of the North Carolina Zoo. As in the other studies, visitors were unobtrusively observed as they viewed exhibits. However, unlike the previous two studies, the position of labels was systematically manipulated so that two or more label positions could be compared at the same exhibit. In some exhibits, the same label was evaluated on the railing in front of visitors as they viewed an exhibit, on the side of the exhibit in a vertical position, and above the exhibit as is common in aquariums. In other exhibits, only the railing and side placements were compared. Finally, in one exhibit (lion), a rear placement was compared with side and railing positions.

Results

Table 11.1 summarizes the study in the Attack & Defense Gallery at the Anniston Museum of Natural History. Clearly, those labels that were placed high above eye level and those that required visitors to turn away from an exhibit to read were attended to much less often than those placed in the overhead; the overhead labels averaged 21.3 percent reading, the two labels in the rear position averaged 30 percent, and the line-of-sight placement labels averaged 65.9 percent reading.

The center of Table 11.1 shows the summary data from the Social Animal Building at the Birmingham Zoo. While there was a lower overall percentage of visitors who appeared to read the labels, the pattern was consistent with the Anniston Museum study in terms of line-of-sight placement being superior to overhead or rear placement.

The bottom of Table 11.1 shows the results from the North Carolina Zoo study. The overhead (6.3 percent reading) and rear (9.0 percent reading) placements were obviously less effective in capturing visitor attention than the railing (31.2 percent reading) or side (28.0 percent reading) placements.

Discussion

The three studies in this report are consistent in showing that visitors attend less frequently to labels that are not within their normal line of sight. Placing labels high above eye level, or in some other position that does not normally

Table 11.1: Label Reading and Placement in Three Exhibition Centers

Attack & Defense: Anniston Museum

Placement	% Read	N	No. Labels
Overhead	21.3	401	3
Line-of-sight	65.9	650	8
Rear	30.0	210	2

Social Animal House: Birmingham Zoo

Placement	% Read	N	No. Labels
Overhead	20.5	639	14
Line-of-sight	33.2	187	4
Rear	10.5	114	2

North Carolina Zoo

Placement	% Read	N	No. Labels
Overhead	06.3	432	3
Line-of-sight	31.2	844	6
Rear	09.0	199	1

capture the visitors' line of sight, can apparently decrease label reading from 10 to up to 40 percent.

Previous studies have found that other physical features of a label (e.g., number of words and length of text) are critical variables for drawing visitor attention (for example, Bitgood, Nichols, Pierce, Conroy, & Patterson, 1986; Borun & Miller, 1980; Thompson & Bitgood, 1988). To this list of variables, position with respect to line-of-sight placement must be added. The best-designed label can languish in obscurity if it is poorly placed. This conclusion is not new. Melton's early work (1972) also demonstrated the importance of both placement of labels and exhibit objects.

Implications

How do you know if your labels are effectively placed? Mock-up or formative evaluation is the best way to check whether or not labels are properly placed (e.g., Screven, 1988). Carefully observing how many visitors attend to a label in two or more positions can ensure that an otherwise well-designed label is effectively placed.

We assume the probability of visitor reading is related to several physical features, each of which has a psychological impact on visitors. Line-of-sight placement is important because of visitors' tendency to attend to objects/labels placed within a limited range around a central visual focus. Objects placed outside this functional zone have a lower probability of detection. Legibility, label length, and text size also have an impact on visitors' perceptions of the possible costs (effort) and benefits of approaching and ultimately reading the label. Visitors are reluctant to read long labels or labels with small lettering, or labels with glare or poor contrast between letter and background because the cost (effort) is too great for the perceived benefit. Finally, the density of labels and objects is likely to influence label reading in two ways: stimulus overload and stimulus detection. Too many labels in proximity to one another make it difficult both to process information and to detect all of the relevant labels.

If this analysis is correct, exhibit labels should be designed so that they:

1. Are placed within the visitors' functional visual zone as they move through an exhibition;
2. Maximize perceived benefits to the visitors for reading while minimizing the perceived effort of reading; and
3. Do not overtax the visitors' ability to process visual information in the exhibition.

NOTE

Previously published as Bitgood, Benefield, & Patterson (1989).

chapter 12

Prompting Attention to Exhibits by Supplementing Audio with Text

▷ **KEY IDEAS** ◁

- For visitors to understand the messages of an exhibition, the purpose of the message must be clear.
- Audio messages must be associated with other exhibit elements to make sense.
- Adding text that mirrored audio messages allowed visitors to understand the message of an exhibition and dramatically increased the viewing time.

Introduction

There are times when exhibition design fails to create the intended experience. Sometimes subtle cues of design do not translate and are lost on the visitor. For example, an exhibit designer was giving me a tour of one of his exhibitions and explained how a slight rise in the floor represented a higher altitude of animal habitat. The cue was too subtle for me until the designer told me, and I am certain visitors rarely saw the connection. When important design intentions are not met, it is important to assess the difficulty and look for a cost-effective solution.

The study reported in this chapter demonstrated how a small, inexpensive change in exhibit design can have a large impact on visitor attention. In the case of the study described in this chapter, adding text to photographs to augment audio messages prompted more engaged attention to exhibit elements as well as improved comprehension of the message. Prior to the written text on the photographs, visitors rarely understood that the amplified voices represented the people in the photographs and that these messages expressed

Attention and Value: Keys to Understanding Museum Visitors by Stephen Bitgood, 137–144.

typical attitudes of people prior to the civil rights movement. The text on the photographs delivered the message more effectively and resulted in considerable more attention to objects in the gallery.

Unfortunately for visitors, a couple of years later, once the lettering started showing its age by starting to peel off, the lettering was removed, and the gallery returned to its original condition.

The Civil Rights Institute

The Civil Rights Institute in Birmingham, Alabama, officially opened its doors on November 16, 1992. Since so many significant events of the civil rights movement for African Americans occurred in the city of Birmingham, it is only fitting that the Institute focuses on Birmingham's civil rights history. However, the Institute also includes descriptions of many other significant events in the civil rights movement, including a gallery on the general issue of human rights. The Institute contains four main galleries: Barriers, Confrontation, Movement, and Human Rights Throughout the World. The second gallery, Confrontation, is the focus of this report.

CONFRONTATION GALLERY. The Confrontation Gallery, a partially darkened room immediately following the Barriers Gallery, consists of 14 life-size black-and-white photos of people on vertical sheets of Plexiglas placed around the room, creating an ambiguous pathway. These visual images are accompanied by recorded voices, randomly coming from different parts of the room, to exemplify the wide range of conflicting attitudes at the beginning of the civil rights movement. Voices can be heard repeating the conflicting attitudes at the time the civil rights movement was about to begin, such as "Separate is equal," and "Don't he know that the colored entrance is around back?" The purpose of these voices is to instill a feeling of tension in the visitor to illustrate the social atmosphere at the beginning of the civil rights movement. On the far wall of the gallery is an outline of a Ku Klux Klan rally with an image of a burning cross. Here also is a well-lit label that says "Bombingham," which describes some of the violent confrontation between the white extremists and blacks.

The Problem and Purpose

Based on an initial evaluation involving self-reports and casual observation, it was believed that the Confrontation Gallery could be further improved by helping to focus attention on the recorded voices and thus make clear what the conflicting attitudes were at the time that the civil rights movement began in the 1950s and 1960s. Visitors appeared to be confused and could not identify which photograph corresponded to which voice. Before the study, visitors tended to walk relatively quickly through this gallery.

The Confrontation Gallery was enhanced by placing written text on the Plexiglas photo panels that corresponded to the audio-recorded statements. Text placement was completed in two phases to assess the possibility that having written text on all panels would create competition for attention and result in less attention to individual panels.

This study could be called "remedial evaluation" (Bitgood & Shettel, 1993; Screven, 1990), since it made changes to a completed exhibition using visitor data as feedback for effectiveness. The technique includes three major steps: (1) collecting visitor data on the exhibition's performance; (2) identifying exhibit elements that do not appear to be performing in an optimal way and make simple, mock-up changes; and (3) collecting additional visitor data to assess the impact of the changes. Evaluation after the exhibition is installed can be particularly effective for identifying and correcting problems that arise when all of the individual elements are put together. Such problems include elements that fail to fall within visitor sight lines, traffic flow problems, and distracting stimuli from other exhibits.

Method

Initially, the gallery consisted of only an introductory panel with text, 12 photo panels with no text arranged in sets of two, and the "Bombingham" label on the back wall (as previously mentioned). Written text was added to the photo panels in two phases. Figure 12.1 is a diagram of the exhibit gallery illustrating the location of the Plexiglas panels and the "Bombingham" label on the back wall.

Recording Procedure: Tracking

The first visitor to enter the gallery was selected and observed until he/she left the gallery. Then, the next visitor to enter the gallery was selected, and so on. As visitors were tracked through the gallery, the following events were recorded: (1) total time in the gallery area; (2) time stopping and viewing Plexiglas photo panels; (3) time spent reading text and labels; and (4) estimated age, race, gender, and number in group.

Rating Scale

Visitors were systematically selected as they departed from the exhibit area according to the following procedure. The first individual to exit the exhibit was approached and asked to complete a short survey about the Confrontation Gallery. When the survey for the first visitor was completed, the next visitor to exit was selected, and the process was repeated. The survey included

12 statements (e.g., "The exhibits are enlightening," "It makes history come to life") as well as demographic information. Each item was rated on the following scale: "Strongly Agree," "Agree," "Neutral," "Disagree," and "Strongly Disagree."

Phases of the Study

BASELINE. Before any text was added to the Plexiglas photo panels, the researchers made observations by tracking visitors through the exhibit gallery from the time they entered until the time they left. Baseline data were collected on three successive Saturdays during the month of May. A total of 42

Figure 12.1: Floor Plan of the Confrontation Gallery

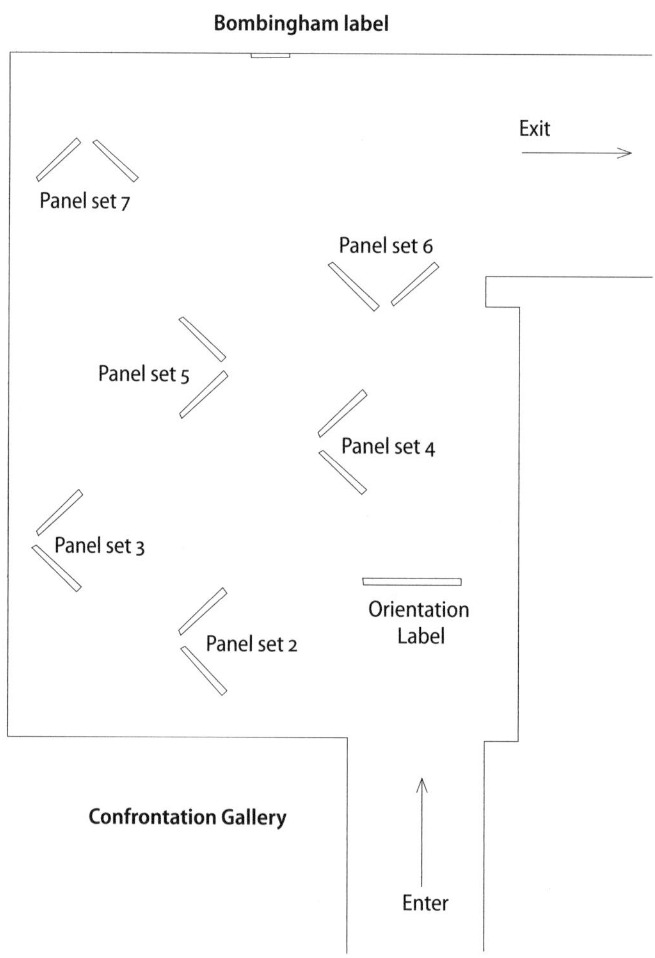

visitors were observed during this phase. In addition, a sample of 51 visitors were given the rating scale to complete.

TEXT-1 CONDITION. Written text labels were placed on five of the twelve photo panels: two on panel set 2, one on panel set 3, one on panel set 4, and one on panel set 7. The written text material corresponded with the voice of the individual making the statement on the overhead audio tape. This condition was in effect on three successive Saturdays during May and June. A total of 84 visitors were observed during this phase.

TEXT-2 CONDITION. Written text labels were placed on all of the remaining Plexiglas photo panels in the gallery. Thus, a total of 12 written statements plus the orientation or introductory statement were present during this phase. Data were collected for three successive Saturdays in June 1994. A total of 54 visitors were observed during this phase. In addition, 75 rating surveys were collected.

Results

Visitor Demographics

Visitors were more likely to be African American (78.5 percent) than white (19.1 percent) or Asian (2.3 percent). Females represented 71.7 percent of the visitor sample. Visitors' ages were distributed across the life span with approximately 40 percent younger than 30 years, more than 42 percent between 30 and 50 years, and the remaining 18 percent older than 50 years. Educational levels were varied: 12.9 percent had not completed high school, 16.2 were high school graduates, 26.7 percent had some college, 21.1 percent were college graduates, and 23.1 percent had a postgraduate education. Two-thirds were part of an organized group and most of the remaining visitors were with family or friends. The percentage of first-time visitors was 88.7 percent. Most visitors came from within a 50-mile radius of the museum.

Tracking Data

Table 12.1 summarizes the tracking data showing significant changes in bold. The observational data clearly show a dramatic impact resulting from placing the text on the photo panels. Total time in the gallery increased dramatically from baseline (24.6 seconds) to the Text-1 condition (78.2 seconds), and finally to the Text-2 condition (117.1 seconds). The percentage of visitors stopping at individual panels and the amount of time stopped also changed dramatically through the study.

Table 12.1: Percentage of Visitors Stopping and Viewing Time During Three Phases of Study

Panel	Baseline	Text-1	Text-2
Intro Panel			
Stop, %	59.5	40.0	**65.7**
View Time, sec	6.9	10.3	**10.4**
Panel Set 2			
Stop, %	14.3	**63.5**	**88.5**
View Time, sec	4.2	**11.6**	**11.3**
Panel Set			
Stop, %	4.8	**35.3**	**60.0**
View Time, sec	3.0	**7.5**	**10.3**
Panel Set 4			
Stop, %	23.8	**63.4**	**77.1**
View Time, sec	4.5	**6.9**	**10.8**
Panel Set 5			
Stop, %	21.4	5.9	**65.7**
View Time, sec	8.9	**6.0**	**6.8**
Panel Set 6			
Stop, %	21.4	7.1	**62.8**
View Time, sec	**3.8**	**4.8**	**7.8**
Panel Set 7			
Stop, %	11.9	**40.0**	**60.0**
View Time, sec	**4.4**	**7.1**	**10.6**
Bombingham			
Stop, %	78.6	84.5	88.5
View Time, sec	18.5	39.5	37.6

Note: Numbers in bold indicate significant difference.

BASELINE CONDITION. Very little time was spent looking at the Plexiglas photo panels or walking through the gallery, with only an average of 29 percent of visitors stopping, and viewing time for the total gallery only averaging 24.6 seconds. When visitors did stop, they remained stationary for very brief periods of time.

TEXT-1 CONDITION. When the written text was placed on five of the twelve panels (see Figure 12.1), the average time viewing these panels rose significantly, with an average of 42 percent of visitors stopping. In addition, total time spent in the Confrontation Gallery (78.7 percent) was more than twice that of the baseline condition. In addition to a dramatic increase in stops at the panels where text was added (50 percent of visitors stopping for an average of 52.2 seconds), there was a decrease in stops at panels on which no text was added (7 percent of visitors stopping for an average of 10.8 seconds). Visitors not only increased attention to exhibit elements with text, they also redistributed their attention so that panels without text received less attention.

TEXT-2 CONDITION. Viewing time and the percentage of visitors stopping continued to increase dramatically. An average of 71 percent of visitors stopped, and average total viewing time was increased to 119.8 seconds. Changes in visitor behavior toward the introductory panel and the "Bombingham" label were also noted. For the introductory panel, the percentage of visitors stopping dropped in the Text-1 condition (40 percent) compared with the baseline condition (59.5 percent) and rose again in the Text-2 condition (65.7 percent). Viewing time showed the opposite pattern, peaking at 10.3 seconds in the Text-1 condition. For the "Bombingham" label, the percentage of visitors stopping increased throughout all conditions, and viewing time peaked again during the Text-1 condition at 39.4 seconds. The reason for these changes is not known. Perhaps increased attention in the total room increased attention on these beginning and ending panels as well, or possibly some other outside manipulations were responsible.

Rating Scale Data

The rating scale data also showed changes from baseline to the Text-1 and Text-2 conditions. Interestingly, before the text was added, visitors reported that the gallery "made me feel more angry" (61.9 percent agree) than after the text was added (55.3 percent agree). The percentage of visitors disagreeing with this statement increased from 14.3 percent before the text addition to 27.6 percent after the text addition. At the same time, agreement with the statement "it makes me feel depressed" increased from 32.8 percent to 48.3 percent. The percentage of agreement with the statement "the experience was emotionally uplifting" decreased from 76.6 percent to 59.0 percent corresponding with the addition of written text. There was also an increase in the percentage of disagreement with this statement associated with the addition of written text. Finally, the statement "I find it difficult to believe that these events really happened" also changed in the amount of agreement-disagreement after the text was added. Percentage of agreement decreased from 24.7 percent to 7 percent, and percentage of disagreement increased from 60.1 percent to 93.1 percent.

Discussion

As shown by this study, a simple change during remedial evaluation significantly influenced the impact of the exhibition gallery. The study demonstrates that small changes in exhibit design can often produce a large change in the pattern of attention within the exhibition. In the Confrontation Gallery, supplementing the audio with written text significantly increased time in the gallery and time viewing each panel. In addition, survey ratings of reactions to this gallery changed. For example, to some extent, feelings of anger appeared to be replaced by feelings of depression.

The increase in the percentage of visitors stopping and the dramatic increase in viewing time from the Text-1 condition (with five written labels) and the Text-2 condition (with twelve text labels) was surprising in light of Melton's (1935) report that increasing pictures in an art gallery resulted in increased competition for visitor attention and ultimately led to decreased attention to each picture. We can only speculate why such competition for visitor attention did not occur in this study. Perhaps in this case, written text more than audio messages provide a better understanding about the gallery's message. Once stopped, visitors are more likely to focus on the educational message.

Since the purpose of the Confrontation Gallery was to create tension by presenting the conflicting attitudes at the beginning of the civil rights movement, the addition of text to supplement audio messages is consistent with the intentions of design. The important point is that effective management of visitor attention requires a carefully examination of how attention is being distributed and making changes when design fails. Even though the study in this chapter was conducted almost two decades ago, it provides a useful approach to identifying and improving problems in visitor attention.

NOTE:

This chapter is based on Bitgood, Cleghorn, Cota, et al. (1996).

chapter 13

Prompting Attention with a Large Interpretive Background

▹ **KEY IDEAS** ◃

- The attention-value model suggests that exhibit design elements can prompt multiple functions: (1) capturing visitor attention; (2) changing the visitor traffic flow; and (3) creating deeper visitor attention engagement.
- The study in this chapter accomplishes all three uses of these functions. The addition of life-sized animal cutouts on the zoo trail led to changes in the visitor traffic flow as well as directed attention to the interpretive message.
- Understanding how exhibit elements can prompt engaged visitor attention can improve outcomes.

Introduction

Arguably, the most common problem in exhibition centers is the visitors' failure to pay attention to exhibits that have the potential to deliver high satisfaction and meaningful information. When visitors do not pay attention to exhibits, possible design shortcomings should be examined. As noted in Chapter 5, exhibit elements may fail to capture attention for several reasons. For example, visitors may not detect the exhibit elements, they may be distracted by more salient, visually competing objects, or the pathway taken may not pass by the exhibit object. This chapter reports on a study in which all of these problems contributed to visitors not paying attention to an observation area overlooking several species of antelope in a zoo. Life-sized silhouettes of different species of antelope were used to prompt attention to distinguishing features of different antelope, to increase the traffic flow to the exhibit overlook, and to engage visitors in interpretive text about the animals.

Attention and Value: Keys to Understanding Museum Visitors by Stephen Bitgood, 145–151.

The purpose of the study in this chapter was to prompt or direct visitor attention to life-sized animal cutouts that revealed the shape and distinctive characteristics of different species of antelope. The cutouts were placed so that once they captured attention, they would visually pull visitors down the pathway leading to the antelope overlook. The size and novel shape of the background provided the necessary characteristics for capturing visitor attention.

The cutouts also served as a background for interpretive labels. The life-sized animal cutouts served to provide visitors with information not available by directly observing the animals. For example, the antelope in the exhibit area must be viewed at a distance, making it difficult to judge their actual size. The size and shape of the cutouts gave visitors a more accurate perception of the animal's actual size. In addition, when multiple species are contained in the same exhibit space, shape identification may occur more easily with the aid of the cutouts.

Method

The exhibit area studied in this project was the African Plains Overlook at the North Carolina Zoo (see Figure 13.1). The Overlook Exhibit area presented several problems commonly found in exhibition centers. First, it required visitors to walk down a trail to a viewing cul-de-sac about 75 feet from the main path. Consistent with previous studies, visitors appeared reluctant to stray off the main path, resulting in a low probability of Overlook trail usage. A second problem with this exhibit was one of animal identification. The Plains Overlook Exhibit contained a number of animals, including several antelope species. Visitors were not able to easily identify the species of animals because of the number of different species on exhibit, the similarity of antelope types, and the large distance between the visitor and the animals. A third problem was the attractiveness of the Elephant Exhibit, which is adjacent to the Overlook. Visitors who had first visited the pavilion exhibit (containing a large number of African animal and plant species) could see the elephants in the distance. A large number of visitors were intent on seeing the elephants from a close distance and were less interested in viewing antelope, a less popular animal than the elephant (e.g., Bitgood, Patterson, & Benefield, 1988). Thus, the attention of visitors coming from the Pavilion was attracted toward the elephants, which competed with viewing the Overlook exhibit.

For the on-site evaluation, recorders observed the circulation patterns as visitors traveled by or on the African Plains Overlook trail. The following events were recorded: the direction of origin (from the African Pavilion or from the elephant exhibit); the pathway taken (main path only or Overlook trail); and reaction to the cutouts (glance, stop, no attention, or did not travel down the Overlook trail). Visitor conversations were also recorded whenever possible. In addition, researchers interviewed a small sample of visitors.

Three animal silhouettes were used: Greater Kudu, Sitatunga, and Thompson's Gazelle. The cutouts were life-sized, and a small label was placed on each cutout. The silhouettes were painted green, the animal outline light green, and the background dark green.

Figure 13.1: Diagram of the Plains Overlook Exhibit

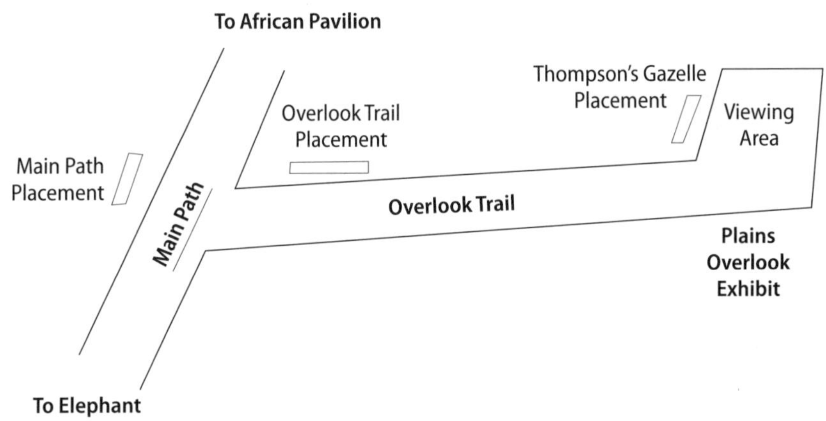

Baseline

During baseline conditions, visitor circulation patterns from both directions were observed, but no animal cutouts were in place. The number of visitors passing along the main path and the number using the Overlook trail were recorded. A total of 325 visitors approaching from the Pavilion and 96 from the elephant exhibit were observed. This difference reflected the uneven traffic flow from the two directions.

First Placement

During this phase, the Sitatunga cutout was placed on the main path (see Figure 13.1), the Greater Kudu cutout was placed on the Overlook trail, and the Thompson's Gazelle was placed in the cul-de-sac area in the rear of Overlook viewing area. A total of 276 visitors were observed during this phase.

After the cutouts were in place, it became apparent that nowhere on the cutout label did it say that the silhouettes represented full-sized animals. In addition, the labels did not direct visitors to the Overlook exhibit area to search for the animals. Thus, during this phase, two labels were added to the Sitatunga label. One label simply stated that the cutout was life-size, and the other label suggested that visitors walk down to the Overlook area and attempt to identify the species.

Cutout Reversal

In a final phase, the positions of the Sitatunga and Greater Kudu cutouts were reversed so that the Kudu was placed on the main path and the Sitatunga was placed along the Overlook Trail. During this phase, 325 visitors were observed.

In addition to the direct observation, a total of 15 visitors were interviewed to determine if the cutouts made it easier to identify the species identified in the labels.

Results And Discussion

Effects of Cutouts on Visitor Circulation

A larger percentage of visitors went down the Overlook trail after the cutouts were in place compared with baseline conditions in which there were no cutouts. The top part of Table 13.1 shows the Overlook trail usage before and after placements of cutouts as a function of the direction from which visitors came. Visitors approaching from the Pavilion were less likely to circulate down the Overlook trail (16.6 percent) before the cutouts were placed than after (25.9 percent). From the elephant exhibit direction, 52.1 percent walked to the Overlook during baseline and 76.5 percent after the cutout placement.

The second part of Table 13.1 shows the percentage of visitors who glanced and stopped as a function of direction of circulation. The most important finding was that the probability of stopping was significantly lower when visitors approached from the Pavilion. About 23 percent of visitors from this direction actually stopped to look at the cutouts. However, visitors approaching from the opposite direction (the elephant exhibit) had a higher probability of stopping (about 32 percent). These results confirm the attracting and distracting power of the elephant exhibit. The elephants' attracting power was too strong for many visitors to engage with the antelopes. Visitors did, however, often glance at the cutouts as they passed by.

Visitor Attention to Cutouts

During the initial placement of the cutouts, visitors were least likely to read the Thompson's Gazelle cutout (5.9 percent stopped to read). The major problem appeared to be its position directly behind the visitor as the visitor viewed the exhibit. Most visitors did not seem to notice its presence, undoubtedly because of its poor location. As indicated in Chapter 11, placement of labels is critical. Reading of the Sitatunga and Kudu labels was in the 20 percent or higher range.

The Effects of Additional Labels

Additional labels were added to the cutouts to point out that the cutouts were life-sized and that they might be able to see these animals from the Overlook. Unfortunately, after observing approximately 200 visitors, we concluded that these supplementary labels had little, if any, effect on the percentage of visitors who walked down the Overlook path or on the percentage of readers. We were not given the opportunity to make additional changes to determine if we could influence more reading and movement how the pathway.

Table 13.1: Attention Data from the Study

Use of Overlook Before and After Cutouts

Origin	Before, %	After, %	Chi-Square
From Pavilion	16.6	25.9	9.086 (*P* = .001)
From Elephant	52.1	76.5	10.150 (*P* = .001)

Visitors Who Glanced and Stopped at Cutouts

Origin	Glance, %	Stop, %
From Pavilion	52.9	22.9
From Elephant	45.6	32.0

Label Reading and Cutout Placement

Path	Sitatunga, %	Greater Kudu, %
Main path	21.6	20.4
Overlook path	30.8	26.3

Stops and Direction of Approach

	Cutout Placement	
Origin	Main Path, %	Overlook Trail, %
From Pavilion	12.4	22.9
From Elephant	38.3	32.0

The Effects of Reversing Cutout Position

The fact that a higher percentage of visitors read the Greater Kudu label than the Sitatunga label could have been due to either the position of the respective cutouts (on the Overlook trail rather than on the main path) or to the cutout characteristics (i.e., size and uniquely shaped horns of the Kudu). The positions of the Kudu and Sitatunga cutouts were reversed so that the Kudu was placed next to the main path and the Sitatunga was placed on the Overlook trail. Once the Greater Kudu and the Sitatunga cutouts were reversed, it was possible to assess the effects of position versus type of species/size of cutout. The third part of Table 13.1 summarizes the effects of cutout position on visitor attention. Visitors were more likely to stop at the cutout if it was placed on the Overlook trail than if it was placed on the main path. The Sitatunga label received slightly more readers than the Kudu label in both placements, although this difference was not statistically significant.

The bottom of Table 13.1 summarizes stops at the cutouts coming from both the main path and the Overlook trail. Again, whether on the main path or on the Overlook trail, visitors were less likely to stop when approaching from the Pavilion due to the high attracting power of the elephants. The probability of stopping on the main path and Overlook trail was higher for visitors approaching from the elephant exhibit area.

Interviews

Interviews confirmed the suspicion that visitors were confused in identifying the various types of antelope, and perceived antelope as less interesting than other species. Visitors also responded favorably to the presence of the cutouts. Although visitors seemed to find the cutouts interesting, zoo staff members offered negative opinions about the cutouts' lack of aesthetic appeal. Some were particularly anxious to remove the cutouts as soon as the study was completed.

Visitors often referred to information contained on the labels when asked what they learned (suggesting they really did read the content). When asked if they thought these cutouts were life-sized, they all responded "yes."

General Discussion

The direction from which visitors approached the cutouts was correlated with whether or not visitors traveled down the Overlook trail. A greater percentage of visitors walked down the trail if they were approaching from the elephant exhibit than from the Pavilion direction. Visitors approaching from the Pavilion appeared to be strongly drawn to the elephants, which were visible as the visitors approached. The total amount of attention (glancing plus stopping) to the cutouts, however, was about equal from both directions. Cutting off the view of the elephants may have had a large impact on attention paid to cutouts.

The addition of the cutouts increased the number of visitors who circulated down the Overlook trail. This suggests that very salient devices such as these life-sized cutouts of large animals provide an effective background for interpretive material, especially when visitors have to be pulled away from the main pathway to view the animals.

Cutouts received more attention (stops) when placed on the Overlook trail than when placed on the main path. Two factors may have accounted for this observation. First, the view with respect to the approaching visitors was better (i.e., the cutouts were angled toward the visitors as they approached). Second, there was less visual competition on the Overlook than on the main path.

Based on hindsight provided by the findings, several improvements could be made. First, the cutouts could be placed in positions to improve the line of sight between visitors and cutout. The angle of placement as well as the specific location play an important role in influencing visitor attention. Second, the prototype labels should have pointed out that the cutouts were life-sized and that the animals might be seen at the Overlook.

This study demonstrated that the cutout design concept is an effective attention-getter. Once the large, novel cutouts capture attention, visitors seem more likely to engage in the interpretive text and more likely to walk down the pathway. The use of large, salient devices like the cutouts can be considered "landmark objects" that, when used effectively, can guide visitor attention.

NOTE

The data for this chapter are taken from Bitgood, Benefield, Patterson, & Litwak (1992).

PART 4

Promoting Engaged Attention Though Exhibit Design

chapter 14

Phenomena Associated with Decreases in Visitor Attention

▹ **KEY IDEAS** ◃

- Several phenomena in museum settings often interfere with paying attention to exhibits.
- Some of these phenomena involve physical or mental states: low energy level, fatigue, and object satiation.
- Others involve perceptual or cognitive processes: selective choice, distraction, and information overload.
- Smart exhibit design can either eliminate or minimize the negative influence of these phenomena on visitor attention.

Introduction

The preceding chapters of this book have been concerned with understanding the mechanisms involved in capturing, focusing, and engaging the attention of visitors. Even when attention is captured and engaged, there are times when a loss of attention may occur. This chapter deals with several phenomena associated with decreased attention. In the past, these phenomena have been often placed under the rubric of "museum fatigue" (Bitgood, 2009a, 2009b, 2009c). However, it is important to make distinctions among several phenomena, three of which are psychophysiological states (low energy level, fatigue, and satiation), two that are sensory perceptual processes (distraction and information overload), and one that is a decision-making process (selective choice).

Descriptions of Phenomena

There are clear distinctions between the various phenomena associated with decreased attention:

Attention and Value: Keys to Understanding Museum Visitors by Stephen Bitgood, 155–165.

- **Low energy level:** a physical-mental condition, acute or chronic, in which the individual feels tired; it may result from illness, lack of sleep, or some type of chronic stress.
- **Acute physical fatigue:** a short-term physical state in which decreased attention results from *prolonged physical exertion over time*, such as walking for several hours without a break, or repeated bending, crouching, and stretching to see objects and/or read exhibit labels.
- **Acute mental fatigue:** a short-term mental state in which decreased attention results from pr*olonged mental exertion over time*, such as successively reading a large number of difficult-to-comprehend exhibit labels and attempting to make sense of the meaning of exhibits.
- **Object satiation:** a mental state in which decreased attention results from *repeated exposure to homogenous stimuli/objects* such as artwork, seashells, sabertooth tiger teeth, or other objects similar to one another; or consuming too much of a good thing too fast.
- **Selective choice:** a decision-making process in which people become more selective (i.e., choose to attend to a smaller proportion of objects) as (1) the number of available objects increases, or (2) the processes of satiation and/or fatigue develop.
- **Information overload:** a perceptual process in which there is an inability to process multiple incoming bits of information because information is coming too fast to pay attention adequately to all of it.
- **Distraction:** (1) the involuntary reaction to pay attention to strong visual or auditory stimuli that pulls attention away from a target object (orienting reflex); (2) giving in to the temptation to view other attractive objects/exhibits that have a high attracting value; and/or (3) to a lesser extent, the detrimental impact on attention of having more than one object to process visually.

These phenomena are likely responsible for some of the more negative aspects of the visitor experience (feeling exhausted, cutting short a museum visit, causing irritability and crankiness, and limiting the amount of learning and enjoyment experienced). In most cases, physical fatigue and information overload seem to play less of a role in attention decrements because most museums visits are not prolonged and visitors usually are in control of how much simultaneous information they deal with. However, satiation, mental fatigue, and selective choice probably occur more than museum professionals realize.

It is important to realize that these phenomena interact with one another. For example, when you are physically or mentally fatigued, you are likely to become more selective in what you pay attention to. In addition, when you are physically fatigued, you more easily become mentally fatigued. The degree to which these phenomena interact may be one reason why they are so difficult to study. This chapter will attempt to examine these phenomena more closely and identify ways of minimizing their negative impact.

The Measurement of Decreased Attention

Two questions immediately arise with respect to loss of attention: (1) What do we mean by decreased attention; and (2) How do we measure it?

WHAT DOES DECREASED ATTENTION MEAN? There are at least two possible meanings associated with attention reduction:

1. **Reduced attention over time.** The first meaning refers to a reduced level of attention compared with some previous high point. When some measure of attention decreases over successive object viewing, we can say that attention is reduced. Such is the case for physical and mental fatigue as well as object satiation. In this case, the reduction in attention becomes more pronounced as viewing time increases.
2. **Reduction in overall level of attention.** Another meaning of decreased attention refers to engaging in a lower level of attention at the very beginning of a museum visit than would have occurred if the phenomenon were not operating. For example, if I have a low energy level from lack of sleep or illness, I might not be able to engage with exhibits at my normal level of attention. In this case, we argue that an object would have received a higher level of attention had not the detrimental process (low energy level) occurred. To assess phenomena such as "selectiveness" and "distraction," we must compare the level of attention with and without the specific condition (e.g., with and without competing objects to choose from, or with single versus multiple distracting objects simultaneously present).

WHAT MEASURES ARE USED TO INDICATE A LOSS OF ATTENTION? Five types of measures have been used to indicate a loss of attention:

1. **Percentage stopping.** One of the most common measures of visitor attention is the percentage of visitors who pass by an exhibit and actually stop and view it rather than walk by. It is important to realize that stopping is a type of choice response. An individual can choose either to stop or not for each exhibit. Failing to stop may be considered indicative of a low level of interest; however, it could also indicate a problem of detection. A poorly placed exhibit object may be given no attention because it is not detected as a result of its placement or because of distracting effects from other objects. Since stopping is an indicator of several processes, we must be careful not to attribute an increase or decrease to one phenomenon.

2. **Viewing time.** Once stopped, how long do visitors view the exhibit? As with stopping, viewing time can be influenced by a number of things, including the processes that are part of fatigue, satiation, and the like.
3. **Self-report.** For the majority of visitor studies found in the literature, self-report data have been used. Ironically, self-report data have been used less frequently as a measure of decreased attention (e.g., fatigue). When self-report is used, the instruments are likely to use rating scales for items such as interest, mental or physical fatigue, and boredom.
4. **Time samples.** Time sampling scores specific behavior outcomes during arbitrary time intervals. Only one study reported time samples of attention during a museum visit (Falk, et al., 1985). Additional use of time samples in visitor research is needed to assess the utility of this approach (see Bitgood [2009a, 2009b, 2009c] for a critique of this method).
5. **Reading.** Reading as a measure of attention decrease has not traditionally been used in studies of decreased attention, although it would seem to be important since reading requires a deeper level of engaged attention than some of the other measures.

Phenomena Associated With Decreased Attention

Energy Level

Lack of sleep, sickness, or recent exertion without rest may all result in a low energy level. I could not find visitor studies (other than a simulated museum study we conducted [Bitgood, Burt, & Dukes, 2009]) that examined the relationship between energy level and paying attention, but it seems it would have an obvious impact. In the study my colleagues and I conducted, participants rated their energy level the day of the study and correlated it with the proportion of text passages they read during the study. The significance of energy level on visitor attention, and how often it becomes an issue in visitor attention, are unknown at this point.

"Museum Fatigue"

"Museum fatigue" has been a difficult phenomenon to define as well as to measure. Definitions have been ambiguous at best and have lacked specificity as to both outcomes and precipitating conditions. Measures of fatigue have varied from the percentage stopping at an exhibit element, to total time viewing, to time sampling the focus of visitor attention, and finally to self-reports of boredom and/or physical or mental tiredness/exhaustion.

To minimize ambiguous, vague use of terminology, concepts associated with attention should be defined in terms of both the causal or precipitating factors (workload, repeated exposure to homogeneous exhibit objects, etc.) and the visitor outcome (decreased percentage of objects given attention over time, decreased viewing time per object over time, etc.) (see Bitgood, 2009a, 2009b, 2009c). As described in this chapter, there is likely to be more than one reason why visitor attention decreases.

Physical fatigue is distinct from mental fatigue. You may become physically fatigued after walking hours and hours in large museums or theme parks. However, it is also possible to become mentally fatigued by mental exertion with little or no physical effort. Reading a large number of difficult-to-understand exhibit labels is likely to cause mental fatigue. I suspect that in museums, mental fatigue is more likely to be a problem than physical fatigue since one rarely reaches a state of physical exhaustion in most museums. On the other hand, a full day of museum visiting is likely to result in physical exhaustion (fatigue).

Despite the lack of evidence, it is difficult to argue that tiredness/exhaustion does not play a role in what has been called "museum fatigue." We have all experienced physical and/or mental exhaustion after a long day at a museum or theme park. Tiredness may be only one of the possible outcomes associated with "fatigue." Other outcomes may include mental distraction, lack of interest, and other similar states. In addition, because extended periods of time may be necessary to produce physical fatigue, it is more difficult to objectively measure in a research study because of the added time needed to study.

Mental fatigue may be easier to demonstrate that physical fatigue. I recently completed a museum simulation study with two of my students (Bitgood, Burt, & Dukes, 2009) in which one group was instructed to describe art prints while another group passively viewed the print. We assumed the mental effort/exertion required in describing the print would contribute to greater mental tiredness/exhaustion than for the group who simply viewed the print. In fact, we did find significantly more participants meeting "fatigue" criteria for viewing time, for rating of interest in the art prints, and for the amount of text passage read.

GENERALIZATIONS. My review of the studies by Gilman (1916), Robinson (1928), and Melton (1935) in Chapter 2 suggest some of the difficulty in studying fatigue. For a critical review of the literature including the methods and findings of other studies, see Bitgood (2009a, 2009b, 2009c). Here are some of the tentative issues and conclusions my colleagues and I have made:

1. Most of the treatments of fatigue in the museum literature appear to have ambiguous and surplus meanings. This is true especially if museum

fatigue is defined only by it its outcome (decreased attention) rather than by a combination of both the cause (contributing conditions) and outcome (behavior).

2. There is a strong misconception among both visitors and museum professionals that museum fatigue is inevitable, and that it cannot be eliminated.

3. Much of what has been called "fatigue" is not really fatigue, but is likely to be satiation and/or selectiveness (a reaction to having multiple objects to attend to at any given moment).

4. Visitors may actively avoid states of fatigue by the choices they make. If you become more selective in what you give attention or if you cut short a visit to one exhibition gallery and go to another, you may minimize or prevent the onset of fatigue.

5. Fatigue is a psychophysiological state that interacts with other processes. For example, we suspect that when visitors experience satiation, they are likely to experience physical and mental fatigue more rapidly. In addition, choosing between and among multiple exhibit elements that constantly compete for attention hastens mental fatigue.

Object Satiation

We have all experienced satiation from consuming too much food. At the end of a large Thanksgiving dinner, you may not want to see turkey again for a long time. However, several hours later your appetite has returned, and you are ready to eat turkey leftovers. Having too much of a good thing (in a short time) is common for many life situations, including viewing exhibits in museums. After consuming many exhibit objects, especially if they are of similar types (all seashells, reptiles), we tend to find ourselves satiated for the moment. It is apparent that satiation occurs for a wide variety of stimulation, including food, play activities, and social contact. Each specific type of stimulus seems to have a different rate of satiation, and the degree and rate of satiation seems to be determined, to some extent, on an individual basis.

Robinson and Melton were perhaps the first to suggest that "object satiation" occurs in a museum setting. Several of their studies focused on apparent processes of satiation.

EVIDENCE FOR OBJECT SATIATION. "Satiation" differs from "mental tiredness/exhaustion" in that in the former, individuals are exposed to objects in a way that fails to stimulate either intellectually or emotionally, while in the latter, individuals are given a heavy mental workload. Decreased attention to homogenous objects across time appears to be a common outcome. Decreased attention can occur with little exertion. For example, it has occurred while a participant viewed art prints while seated at a table (Robinson, 1928) or viewed snakes within a small exhibition space (Bitgood, Patterson, & Benefield, 1986).

GENERALIZATIONS. A review of the literature suggests the following:

1. Satiation is most likely to occur in exhibitions with objects of similar characteristics (paintings of only one genre, seashells, snakes, pottery, etc.) presented with similar design features. Variety of design and variety of objects are likely to minimize satiation.
2. Satiation may differ from fatigue in that: (1) it occurs more rapidly than fatigue; (2) it may occur with minimal expended effort; and (3) it has more rapid recovery. If decreased attention happens after viewing only a handful of objects, it is likely to be satiation rather than fatigue. On the positive side, it doesn't take long to recover from satiation (e.g., move to another exhibit area).

Selective Choice

Melton believed that object competition caused perceptual distraction. However, I believe there is a second type of competition, according to my research, more powerful than perceptual distraction (Bitgood, 2009a, 2009b, 2009c; Bitgood, Burt, & Dukes, 2010). I call this "selective choice" or "selectiveness." As the number of choices available at any moment increase, visitors become more selective in what they choose. They are likely to choose higher-value (utility/cost) alternatives rather than attend to those perceived as having lower interest and higher cost. If you walk into an exhibit gallery and there is only one object, you are very likely to view it. If the same gallery is suddenly filled with many other objects, you can be more selective and focus on those that are perceived to have the highest potential interest and lowest time and effort.

One way to distinguish selectiveness from perceptual distraction is to control choices. If you are given a choice from among 10 objects as to what to view, the selectiveness mechanism will be at work. On the other hand, if you are told which one of 10 objects to give attention (no choice), the processes associated with perceptual distraction are likely to be at work.

Two of my students and I recently completed a museum simulation study using art prints in a laboratory (Bitgood, Burt, & Dukes, 2009). This study examined several factors, including "mental fatigue" outcomes. The study was similar to Robinson's (1928) laboratory study and one of our past studies (Bitgood, Devia, Goodwin, et al., 2001). However, unlike the other studies, three measures of fatigue were examined over the course of the session: (1) viewing time, (2) interest rating of each art print, and (3) the proportion of a text passage read. Half of the participants were instructed to describe the art print as they initially viewed it; the rest of participants simply viewed as long as they wished. All participants were then asked to rate the print in terms of "how interested would you be in seeing information about this artwork and its artist?" Finally, participants were shown a text passage and instructed to read as much or as little as they desired. Results indicated that (1) the vast majority of participants showed signs of "mental fatigue" (as indicated by decreased viewing time, interest rating, and/or proportion of the passage read) across trials of the study, and (2) the participants who had to describe the print showed a higher amount of "mental fatigue" or systematic decreases in the three measures. Obviously, physical exertion was not a factor in this study. However, mental exertion (having to describe the art print) was present since the "describe" condition resulted in greater "mental fatigue" than the "view only" condition.

Unfortunately, there has been little concern about the equivalence of these various "fatigue" measures. I have identified some potential difficulties with some of the methodology in my recent articles (Bitgood, 2009a, 2009b, 2009c). At the very least, the pattern of findings in the literature suggests that different measures are sensitive to different variables.

Perceptual Distraction and Information Overload

Melton (1935) argued that every object competes for attention with every other object that is visually available at any moment. Melton (and Robinson, 1928) believed that object competition had a perceptually distracting impact on attention; that is, the mere presence of alternative objects created a distraction, presumably because of the nature of human sensory-perceptual processes.

Information overload, a concept somewhat similar to distraction, is another phenomenon sometimes confused with "fatigue." Overload is similar to competition in that it may involve simultaneous presentation of multiple objects. Overload can be defined as an inability to process the amount of incoming information. Information is coming in too fast to process. However, in most cases, visitors are able to control the rate at which exhibit information is processed (unless some device such as a video is controlling the rate of information delivery). Matamoros (1986) titled her thesis "Information Overload," but did not actually provide an "overload" measure since there was no attempt to control the amount of information presented at one time. Rather, she examined attention (percentage of stopping and viewing time) to exhibits over the course of the aquarium visit. She also collected self-report data of fatigue-like experiences from an independent group of visitors.

GENERALIZATION. While perceptual distraction and/or information overload may occur in exhibit settings, they do not appear to produce as strong an effect as selectiveness (see next section).

Minimizing The Loss Of Attention

There are two approaches to minimizing the loss of paying attention: by design and by personal action. I hope that exhibition developers will incorporate principles that reduce fatigue, satiation, etc. However, even if designers neglect to apply design solutions, visitors might be encouraged to be proactive and use their own resources to reduce attention loss.

Solving the Problem by Design

Each phenomenon must be considered somewhat independently since there are different conditions involved with each.

1. **Energy level.** Design that reduces the workload on all visitors should help relieve much of the burden for visitors who arrive at the museum with a low energy level.[1] Having places to rest distributed throughout the museum also offers a period of sitting to recover.
2. **Mental fatigue** is also reduced by keeping the mental workload to a minimum. This reduced workload includes the effort in processing information from the exhibitions and the effort it takes to navigate through the museum. Concise interpretive labels, bulleting text material, and organizing information for easy mental processing are some of the ways to reduce mental effort.
3. **Physical fatigue** can be minimized by eliminating the necessity to backtrack to view all the exhibit displays and by minimizing the amount of walking, stretching, and other forms of physical exertion necessary to experience the exhibitions. Again, places to take a break and relax also help.
4. **Object satiation** can be minimized by reducing the amount of homogenous objects and exhibit elements. Instead of displaying redundant examples of objects such as seashells, paintings, or stuffed birds, keeping the number of similar objects at a minimum and displaying the objects in varied and interesting ways will help prevent satiation. Provoking greater thought and interest by the way text passages are written is also important for reducing the boredom associated with satiation. Having a snack bar or café for a coffee or soft drink break can help recover visitors' appetite for more exhibits.
5. **Selectiveness** (paying attention to a smaller proportion of exhibits when the number of available exhibits is high) is a way for visitors to choose only those exhibits that promise the highest value. The best way to minimize selective choice of exhibits is to keep the total number visually available at any moment to a minimum. Avoid the open-gallery approach where all objects are visually available at the same time. The open-floor

design practice of science centers often creates needless distraction, especially in young children, who often move frantically from one device to another with minimal "minds on" activity.

6. **Distractions** can be minimized by ensuring that sounds and movements from outside the target exhibit do not cause automatic orienting responses. Sound bleeding from other exhibit displays is a frequent but unnecessary problem. In addition, if distracting movement from other sources is a problem, visual access to these movements can be minimized by good design. Again, it helps to avoid open galleries where sights and sounds from outside a target exhibit might compete for attention. Controlling visual access should be a major consideration in exhibition design.

Solving the Problem by Personal Action

In talking with visitors it is obvious that many already take steps to minimize the phenomena that produce decreased attention. Visitors should be encouraged to take breaks for coffee, snacks, or lunch. Visitors can also be encouraged to sit down and rest occasionally before they become fatigued. Having the café/snack bar in a convenient place helps encourage visitors to take a break. If visitors actively engage with exhibits, satiation may be minimized. When my wife and I are visiting a museum with exhibits that do not interest us, we often try to make up interpretive material for the exhibit objects. This strategy often results in thinking about exhibit objects in more meaningful ways than we might otherwise do. And, it can be fun.

One way to empower visitors is to provide a handout of suggestions that addresses ways to avoid the phenomena that result in attention reduction. Chapter 9 reviews self-guide studies that increase visitor attention. These guides put more control in the hands of the visitor.

Conclusions

After almost a hundred years of studying "museum fatigue" and related phenomena, we know relatively little. The total number of studies addressing these phenomena can be counted on three or four hands (less than 20).

1. The findings from studies are often inconsistent and conflicting.
2. There is a lack of theories or models that give up predictive validity.
3. All observational measures are not the same; there is often poor correlation among them, and some measures are more predictive of specific outcomes.
4. Observational measures do not always agree with self-report measures.

Unfortunately, the complexity and impact of these phenomena appear to be underappreciated. Few researchers and evaluators have attempted to study these concepts. The phenomena discussed in this chapter should be defined by their operations (what conditions must occur, and what outcome measures do we observe?). We need more detailed, logical analysis of these phenomena as well as more research. The studies that my colleagues and I have initiated will hopefully stimulate additional research, if only to attempt to prove us wrong.

NOTE

1. We applaud the Universal Design movement, which is consistent with our own approach. Everyone benefits when all visitors are considered.

chapter 15

Visitor Navigation and Attention

▷ **KEY IDEAS** ◁

- Visitor attention is deeply intertwined with orientation and circulation (collectively called "navigation").
- Efficient movement through complex museum spaces involves a sophisticated navigation system.
- Careful design of navigation systems ensures that visitors do not waste attention resources on orientation and circulation, but instead will be able to enjoy the exhibitions and programs with undivided attention.

Introduction

Navigation and Visitor Attention

In addition to ensuring that visitors engage with exhibitions and programs, managing visitor attention includes helping people navigate through the museum. How visitors navigate determines what they see and do and ultimately what they experience and learn. Effective navigation systems include the capture of attention (detection of navigation cues), focus of attention on important cues (narrowing attention to maps and orientation text material), and engaging attention on relevant navigation cues (e.g., reading text and maps). If visitors do not read or understand the navigation messages, orientation and wayfinding will not work effectively.

What Is Navigation?

Navigation is a combination of orientation and circulation. More formally, we can define visitor navigation as: *the act of moving through the museum in an efficient way; with the knowledge of where you are, where you are going, and*

Attention and Value: Keys to Understanding Museum Visitors by Stephen Bitgood, 166–175.

where to find specific locations; and with a general understanding of what you might experience (e.g., exhibitions, programs) during your visit.

Efficient movement through the museum means that it can be accomplished with minimal time and effort considering the size of the area to be navigated. Inefficient movement is more likely to occur in a mazelike museum where the individual must constantly decide which of many alternative pathways to take and/or under conditions where the individual must repeatedly double back to see all the exhibits. Movement through the museum is called visitor circulation.

Knowledge of physical locations within the museum means that you understand how the facility is organized, you know where you are, where you are going, and where to find specific locations such as the restroom, the café, and the museum store. This type of knowledge is called wayfinding and also includes part of conceptual orientation (how the museum is organized).

A *general understanding of experiences to be encountered* includes what there is to see and do and the general educational meanings found in the museum. These meanings are often simply communicated as the title of an exhibition (The Story of Dinosaurs, or Life on the African Plains). This element of navigation encompasses much of what we call "conceptual orientation."

A *navigation device* is something that aids the act of navigation. Obvious devices include direction signs and maps (fixed or handheld). Less obvious devices include visual access to a location and pathway characteristics. (e.g., number of pathways and intersections within the museum). A *navigation system* is the collection of navigation devices that are available to use by those who visit the museum.

Ideally, a well-designed navigation system provides the opportunity to move through a museum with minimal frustration and effort and maximum satisfaction and reward in what the visitor experiences. Unfortunately, navigation systems in museums are too often inadequate to meet the orientation and circulation goals of visitors. Consideration of visitor orientation and circulation by decision-makers should be a critical part of the functioning of any museum (e.g., Bitgood, 2006, 2011a). For additional information, see my review paper (Bitgood, 2006) and the section of my book on orientation and circulation (Bitgood 2011a, pp. 316–443).

Three Elements of Navigation

Navigation includes three elements:

- **Conceptual orientation** provides information describing what the exhibition is about, how it is organized, and what there is to see and do.

Part of the function of conceptual orientation is to provide an advance organizer so that the visitor group understands the key ideas of the exhibition and allow them to plan their visit. When visitors know what the exhibition is about and how it is organized, they are more likely to plan their movements and engage their attention with material that encourages learning (e.g., Bitgood & Tisdal 1996; Screven, 1986).

- **Wayfinding.** Wayfinding devices provide information that allows visitors to know where they are and how to find their way with minimal effort. This includes knowing how to find locations such as specific exhibits, restrooms, and food, and knowing one's location in relation to other places such as the museum lobby.
- **Circulation.** How visitors move through the built environment can have a significant impact on the visitor experience. Movement through museums is clearly tied to wayfinding. If the exhibition environment is difficult to navigate, confusing in terms of where to go next, and requires unnecessary effort (such as backtracking) to see all of the exhibit displays, the visitor will either refuse to engage in the necessary effort or will expend excessive energy and experience rapid fatigue leaving less attention available to engage with exhibition and program content.

The Importance of Navigation

An effective system of orientation-circulation reduces the workload for visitors so they do not have to expend time and energy trying to understand navigation clues, what to do, where to go, etc. An effective system also ensures that all exhibit displays and elements are given a chance to be detected or noticed. Typically, in an ineffective system, the circulation pattern in exhibitions result in "hot" and "cold" spots with respect to visitor attention. While some of this may be due to varying interest levels of the exhibits, much of it is also the result of poorly designed navigation systems. Paying attention to some exhibit elements and not others often occur because of: (1) design that produces too much object competition or requires backtracking to see all the elements; (2) sight lines that do not include exhibit elements (e.g., two-sided exhibits); (3) unnecessary intersections with multiple choice points that may also confuse visitors, require expending mental effort, and/or result in sections of the exhibitions that are missed entirely. Readers can find additional readings on visitor navigation in *Social Design in Museums: The Psychology of Visitor Studies* (Bitgood, 2011a, pp. 316–443).

Conceptual Orientation

Conceptual orientation should communicate the main ideas of the exhibition and provide enough information for the visitor to plan his/her visit. It provides an advance organizer for the museum visitor and for each exhibition within the museum. Conceptual orientation allows visitors to better plan their visit and to understand what they will encounter during their visit.

Elements of Conceptual Orientation

To capture and engage visitor attention, introductory information should include:

1. **Main ideas.** What is the exhibition all about? Does the title or a short statement communicate the main idea or ideas?
2. **What is there to see and do?** Does the orientation convey what the visitor will see and what activities are available in the exhibition?
3. **How is it organized?** Is there a graphic representation (i.e., a map) of how the exhibition is organized? Is the organization obvious from visual inspection?
4. **Where to find. . . .** Information about the location of restrooms, café, gift shop, lockers or other amenities should also be provided.

Principles of Design

1. All four elements described here should be included in each device for conceptual orientation.
2. Conceptual orientation should be provided for the entire museum (usually placed in the lobby), for each exhibition, and sometimes for groups of exhibits with a common theme within an exhibition.
3. The placement, text length, and font size should follow three basic principles of good design: placed where it is needed; concise and relevant; and large enough font to be easily read.
4. Line-of-sight placement of text and direction signs increases the chance that they will be detected.
5. Minimize competing objects, signs, or other kinds of visual clutter so that the navigation cues will be easily detected.
6. Conciseness: keep messages as brief as possible.

Example

The exhibition *Evolution of Style,* from the Royal Ontario Museum in Toronto, serves as an example of good conceptual orientation (see Figure 15.1). Note

Figure 15.1: Conceptual Orientation for the Royal Ontario Museum's *Evolution of Style* Exhibition

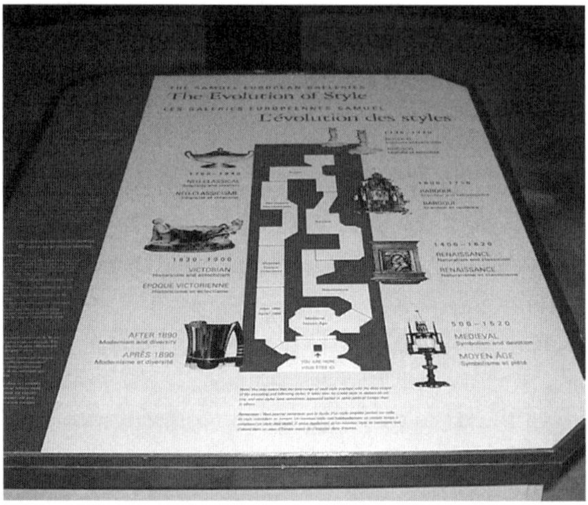

that the map shows clearly how the exhibition is organized. In addition, key exhibit areas inform visitors of the main ideas/content of the exhibition.

Wayfinding (Physical Orientation)

Visitors should not have to invest substantial time and energy finding their way. Locating key areas of a museum should be as effortless as possible. How much time and effort are required to navigate through the exhibition? Is there an explicit system that is easily followed by visitors?

Wayfinding aides include:

1. **Direction signs.** Are direction signs placed in a location where they are needed (e.g., entrances and intersections)? Do they provide clear directions? Are they effective at capturing visitor attention? Do the wayfinding signs get lost among a mixture of other types of signage?
2. **Maps.** You-Are-Here (YAH) maps should also be positioned where they are needed. In addition, they should follow Levine's (1982) principles:
   a. **Forward-up equivalence:** up on the map should be forward in the environment.
   b. **Two points of information:** a location on the map should visually correspond with a location in the environment.

c. **YAH symbol:** a YAH symbol should allow visitors to see where they are in relation to points on the map.

d. **Simplicity:** only necessary information should be contained on the map to minimize confusion.

3. **Museum guides.** Do guides provide basic information (e.g., a map of facility, brief summary of big ideas, what there is to do and see, where to find amenities) that visitors need to plan their visit and navigate through the museum?

4. **Visual access.** Can the visitor see key locations (e.g., signage, objects) from the entrance or other locations within the exhibition? More visitors will travel down a pathway to an exhibition or café if they can see it at a distance (e.g., Bitgood, Benefield, Patterson, & Litwak, 1992). Casinos on the Las Vegas strip deprive their patrons of visual access to what is outside the casino areas, presumably so they are not tempted to leave the casino (Bitgood, 2003). Whenever possible, provide visual access to allow visitors to see down pathways.

Example

A good wayfinding system usually includes more than one of these aides. It is important to provide the necessary information at the location where it can be best used. At the St. Louis Science Center (Bitgood & Tisdal, 1996), Carey Tisdal and I examined a combination of fixed maps, the museum guide with a handheld map, and direction signs at intersections. An orientation device was added to the lobby that included three panels: what to do, where to go, and a map of the Science Center.

Circulation Pathway System

Movement through a museum is more effortless when designed with simple patterns that allow easy formation of a cognitive map of the facility. For example, it is likely easier to navigate a square-shaped main pathway with a few side pathways than a maze of pathways and intersections that are not clearly defined. As noted above, in a previous publication (Bitgood, 2003), I compared museums with Las Vegas casino design, where confusing designs are apparently intentional. Below are a few characteristics of facility design that influence ease of circulation:

1. **Complexity of pathways.** Multiple pathways through an exhibition cause confusion and force visitors to squander their time and energy on making decisions about which way to go.

2. **Number of intersections.** Intersections or choice points require decision-making effort that may reduce the energy level for paying attention to exhibition content.
3. **One-sided viewing.** Are there competing exhibits on both sides of the pathway that encourage only one-sided viewing since visitors rarely backtrack?
4. **Turning at intersections.** Is the circulation pathway designed for taking the fewest steps when turning at intersections?
5. **Landmark objects.** Are landmark objects (those that easily capture attention) used to guide visitor attention?
6. **Proximity of elements to visitor.** Are visitors able to move close to the exhibit objects and interpretive text?
7. **Straight versus curved pathways.** Pathways that are curved create two problems: they make it more difficult to formulate a cognitive map of the facility, and they limit visual accessibility (a valuable cue for what is in the environment).
8. **Only 90-degree intersections.** Pathway intersections that are not at a 90-degree angle create problems in formulating cognitive maps of an area. Rounded walls also make it difficult to form a cognitive map of an area.

Some Lessons Learned From Research Projects

Below are brief accounts of a few of our studies that illustrate the principles of navigation discussed in this chapter.

Lobby Orientation

At the St. Louis Science Center, Carey Tisdal and I (Bitgood & Tisdal, 1996) found that when visitors were given museum guides with maps of the facility and brief descriptions of the exhibit areas, they stayed longer and rated their overall visitor satisfaction higher than visitors who did not have a guide with a map. In addition, a lobby orientation device was tested that provided necessary information for navigation, including what there was to see and do, a map showing how the Center was organized, and where to find key locations. Visitors who used this device were more likely to report that they had enough information to plan their visit than did nonusers.

Handheld Maps

Visitors at the Birmingham (AL) Zoo were tracked from the time they entered until they exited the zoo (Bitgood & Richardson, 1987). Half of the visitors were given a handheld map of the zoo; the other half did not have a map. When visitors had maps, most (77 percent) were observed using them, and those with maps viewed 86 percent of the zoo's exhibits; those without maps viewed 78 percent of the exhibits. Since many of the visitors from both groups were repeat visitors, the impact of handheld maps might have been greater if the study had been conducted exclusively with first-time visitors.

Fewest-steps Principle

The value principle (from the attention-value model) argues that the lower the cost in terms of time and effort, the higher the value of a response. Visitors choose to do things that reduce cost as much as possible. When navigating through a museum, one way to reduce cost is to take the fewest number of steps possible. Several pedestrian patterns are consistent with the fewest-steps principle; these observations are consistent with the visitor studies literature (Bitgood, 2006). The fewest-steps principle also predicts that at intersections, pedestrians should choose to turn right, turn left, or go straight ahead based on how many steps are required. If a pedestrian is walking on the right side of a pathway, turning right or going straight ahead requires fewer steps than turning left from the right side of the pathway. We and others have validated this prediction in studies of pedestrians in shopping malls (Bitgood & Dukes, 2006; Bitgood, Davey, Huang, & Fung, 2012; Spilkova & Hochel, 2009).

"Burma-Shave" Orientation Signs

In this study, we adopted a lesson from the old Burma Shave road signs of many years ago (see Sedlmaier 2012 for reference). These signs were brief statements advertising Burma Shave spread out sequentially along the highway over a distance of miles. At the time of this study (Bitgood, Benefield, & Patterson, 1987), the Space & Rocket Center in Huntsville, AL, offered several choices of tickets: museum visit only, NASA bus tour, Omnimax film, or a combination of choices. Total time of participation for these alternatives was a problem if the visitor wished to participate in multiple events. For example, the bus tour was almost two hours long and the Omnimax film was ninety minutes long. Visitors frequently were not aware of the time requirements and often purchased tickets for more activities than budgeted time allowed. It was clear from interviewing a few visitors before and after they purchased tickets that many did not understand what type of ticket they had purchased and how long the activities would take.

We placed a series of signs ("Burma Shave"–style) along the sidewalk as visitors approached the lobby. Each sign briefly indicated the activity (film, museum, bus tour) and how long each would take. When visitors reached the ticket line after reading these simple signs, they were more able to make a knowledgeable choice of which type of ticket to purchase. They also spent less time at the ticket counter since the ticket options did not have to be explained as they purchased their ticket.

Las Vegas Casino Design Principles

While attending conferences for several years in a row in Las Vegas, I noticed that the design of the casino areas in the large hotels on the Strip was inconsistent with the design of the shopping areas that often accompany them (Bitgood, 2003). Shopping areas tended to have few pathways or choices to make at intersections. Shoppers had easy visual access to what was ahead. As with most shopping malls, navigating through the shopping area did not take much time and effort. The casino areas, on the other hand, appeared to use the same design principles, but in reverse. Pathways were complex and rarely straight with 90-degree intersections. Visual access to areas outside the gambling area was nonexistent (including the hotel registration desk in several cases).

I don't know if casinos actually have data that show patrons gamble more when they are confused, but given the financial outcome involved, they must know what they are doing.

A Study of Changing Exhibits in a Gallery

To assess the influence on visitor attention of how exhibit displays are arranged within an exhibit hall, we conducted a tracking and timing study in several different temporary exhibitions over a period of 12 months (Bitgood, 2011a; Bitgood, Hines, Hamberger, & Ford, 1991). The pathway through the exhibition changed dramatically depending upon the spatial arrangement of exhibits. Island displays presented a problem for visitors in that there was no clear pathway through the exhibition hall to see all of the exhibits, resulting in "hot" and "cold" areas of attention. In an exhibition of stroboscope-produced photographs by Edgerton, 6 of 14 photos on island displays received 50 percent or more stopping, while 11 of 13 photos on the wall received the same level of attention. Many of the island-placed photos that received little or no attention were on the opposite side as visitors approached, suggesting the importance of sight lines in capturing attention.

Concept Orientation and the Title of Exhibition Area

In one of our studies at the Anniston Museum of Natural History, we suspected that visitors were having difficulty associating the name of the exhibition area with exhibits within the area (Bitgood & Patterson, 1987). We asked visitors to match specific exhibits with the exhibition area in which they could be found. Out of 20 exhibit names, visitors could only place four in their correct exhibition areas. The problem was that the exhibition area titles (e.g., Designs for Living) did not immediately convey the meaning of the exhibition (Designs for Living referred to the Bird Hall). At least one aspect of concept orientation is improved when the names of the objects can be easily placed into the exhibition area.

chapter 16

Visitor Attention in Exhibitions: Some Guiding Principles

▷ **KEY IDEAS** ◁

- Evaluation is an important aspect of exhibition development, including its postinstallation life. Evaluation of how visitors distribute their attention and what they learn and experience is needed to assess success.
- Visitor navigation should be integrated with other aspects of exhibit design from the very start rather than as an afterthought.
- Attention in exhibitions can be examined within exhibits (focus on the organization and layout of exhibit elements within a display) and between exhibits (e.g., physical organization of exhibit displays within the exhibition space, sight lines, and pathway through the exhibitions).
- Within- and between-exhibit attention include different sets of person-setting and response-impact variables.

Introduction

Whether or not explicitly stated, every exhibit designer/developer has his/her own theory of visitors. These theories are often incomplete because they fail to incorporate the psychology of managing visitor attention. All viewpoints should include an understanding of psychological factors that influence navigation, detection of exhibit elements, and the motivation for engaging attention.

Good exhibition design manages visitor attention in a manner that is often subtle, that provides visitors with high value experiences, and that minimizes unwanted outcomes such as fatigue, satiation, and distractions. Good design is subtle in that the visitors may not be consciously aware of the manner in which they are guided by sight lines, circulation pathways, and other cues

Attention and Value: Keys to Understanding Museum Visitors by Stephen Bitgood, 176–183.

that allow movement with minimal effort through the exhibition. High-value experiences are provided by maintaining high visitor interest, curiosity, and satisfaction while minimizing the time and effort required to have a satisfying experience. Physical and mental fatigue are controlled by minimizing physical and mental effort, by reducing the frustrations of wayfinding and of having difficulty understanding the intended messages of the exhibition. Good design also avoids repetitive, boring stimulation that creates object satiation. In addition, good design minimizes sensory distractions (such as sounds from other extra-exhibit sources) and competing visual elements that pull attention away from important exhibit elements.

The current chapter provides a guide for managing visitor attention based on the attention-value model. The guide is designed to provide assistance in the process of analyzing how exhibitions influence or fail to influence visitor attention. The chapter attempts to conceptually organize under the rubric of the attention-value model what we know about visitor research in a way that helps to identify strengths and weaknesses of exhibitions and suggests cost-effective ways to improve their overall visitor impact. The items in the guide identify many of the most important factors that influence the management of visitor attention. Based on a three-stage analysis of visitor attention (capture, focus, and engagement), the guidelines were designed to organize the visitor research literature in a way meaningful to users. The relevance of these factors will, of course, vary from exhibition to exhibition, but in general, the same factors appear to influence visitor attention across types of exhibitions, types of museums, and types of visitors.

Much of this book has focused on the processes, variables, and supporting evidence involved in the management of visitor attention in museum exhibitions. This chapter provides a summary of this information and offers guidelines for incorporating the most important principles in attention management.

Evaluation

In the last half-century, numerous evaluation studies have demonstrated, beyond any reasonable doubt, the power of applying evaluation methods to the exhibition development process.[1] Today, there are many resources available, including evaluation guides (Frechtling 2010) as well as examples of evaluations.[2]

Systematic visitor input is useful during all three major stages of exhibit development: planning, preparation, and postinstallation. A review of the visitor literature can help guide the exhibition development process by providing successful examples on topics similar to the project in question. Briefly, the types of evaluation that have proven useful during exhibition development include:

1. **Front-end evaluation.** During the planning stage of an exhibition, a front-end survey can be helpful to assess visitor interests, media preferences, and preknowledge associated with a topic (Borun, 1990).
2. **Formative evaluation.** Trial testing mock-ups of exhibit displays is a valuable way to ensure that the messages are clear and that visitors understand what to do. The test-retest methodology of formative evaluation identifies what works and what doesn't and allows immediate testing of solutions when exhibits do not perform as desired.
3. **Critical appraisal.** An assessment of an installed exhibition by a knowledgeable, objective professional who critiques the exhibition based on findings from the visitor literature can identify possible strengths and weaknesses of an exhibition. Some problems (e.g., excessively long interpretive labels) can be easily corrected and do not require collecting visitor data to know that they will not be effective. Potential problems such as clarity of message can be identified and used as the basis for a remedial evaluation.
4. **Remedial evaluation.** After installation of an exhibition, additional evaluation can help further improve its impact on visitors. A critical appraisal should lead to possible problem areas that require visitor evaluation to correct. A remedial evaluation can be performed in which these potential exhibition problems are identified and improvements made.

Navigation

The importance of navigation (described in Chapter 15) cannot be overemphasized. Assessing the navigation system can lead to finding areas where conceptual orientation, wayfinding, and circulation can be improved, resulting in more attention and a deeper level of visitor engagement with exhibits. Appendix B (Checklist for Managing Visitor Attention) provides more details on these guidelines, which are summarized here:

1. **Navigation messages should be easy to detect and have value to the visitor at the location they are placed.**
   a. **Detection.** Easy detection occurs when information is placed in a location where it is needed (e.g., at choice points) and where it falls within the visitor line of sight, has good contrast with background, and does not compete with other objects.

b. **Value.** Visitors need information at locations where navigation decisions must be made. The information should be delivered in a way that requires minimal time and effort to extract and process.

2. **Conceptual orientation is included in the navigation system.** This is critical when the subject matter can be misconstrued and/or when the setting has a complex structure. Conceptual orientation is placed both at the museum entrance (in the museum lobby) and at the entrance of each exhibition. Visitors are told what the museum or exhibition is all about, how it is organized, and where to find the restrooms, café, and museum store.
3. **Wayfinding devices follow the suggested guidelines regarding content, placement, and other aspects of design.** These devices include YAH (You-Are-Here) maps following Levine's principles described in Chapter 15 and visitor guides or handheld maps that are available, effectively designed, and consistent with other navigation devices.
4. **The system of pathways and intersections through an exhibition should be as simple as possible and, ideally, easy for a visitor to form a mental map of the museum and each exhibition.** The fewer the pathways and choices at intersections, the fewer choices and less energy expended on navigation. Straight pathways, 90-degree angles at intersections, and visual access down a pathway make it easier to navigate. Pathway systems that form familiar patterns (e.g., circle, square, figure eight) make it easier for visitors to develop an accurate cognitive map of the facility.

Attention To Exhbitions

We can examine the distribution of attention within exhibitions in two ways: within a single exhibit display (within-exhibit factors), and/or between exhibits. When individual exhibit displays are organized into a series of exhibit experiences (between-exhibit variables) a different set of guiding principles must be considered.

It can be highly beneficial to conduct a symbolic "walk-through" assessment of an exhibition model to predict how design characteristics will influence visitors. Possible problems can be quickly identified and design solutions found before a large investment of time, effort, and money.

In general, for both within- and between-exhibit factors, detection and value play an important role in visitor attention. Detection is influenced by the salience of an exhibit object as well as value. The variables discussed in Chapter 5 should be examined.

Within-Exhibit Considerations

The design of each exhibit display has important implications for capturing and engaging visitor attention. The exhibit elements selected, the interpretation provided, and the organization or arrangement of these exhibit elements will influence the pattern or distribution of visitor attention.

DETECTION. The ease of detecting objects and exhibit elements strongly influences how an exhibit is experienced. The visitor is bombarded with stimuli (exhibit elements) in most exhibit environments. Some of these exhibit elements will be detected, but some may not be. Visitors can be easily confused as to what and where they should pay attention. Appendix B lists the most important factors that influence how detectable an exhibit object or element might be. Briefly, these fall into the following factors:

1. **Salience.** Stimuli that are large, moving, have good contrast with the background, fall easily within the visitor line of sight, and that are close to the visitor are most likely to be detected.
2. **Value.** Since visitors are searching for something of high value, exhibit elements that promise high benefit or satisfaction with low cost (time and effort) are most likely to be approached and viewed.

SEQUENCE OF SEARCHING. The pattern of visually processing exhibit elements will determine which ones receive attention, how engaged visitors become, and what messages the visitor takes away from the experience. Visual processing can be sequential or simultaneous. Sequential searching is more likely to result in a systematic and thorough examination of the exhibits. Simultaneous processing is more likely to result in selective attention to only the most salient of exhibit elements. In a simultaneous or parallel search, the visitor waits for something salient to "pop out" of the exhibit. In such cases, only the most salient exhibit elements are likely to be given attention.

Visitors use both simultaneous and serial processing. When an environment is first searched, people scan for a salient object to capture attention (simultaneous processing). Three-dimensional, concrete objects are usually the first things that attract attention. Once attention is focused on an object, visitors tend to search in a serial fashion (systematically search one element after another) for interpretative information about the object. Brandy New and I recently completed a study that supported this observation (Bitgood & New, 2012).

VALUE. While the processes of detection are critical during the capture of attention, the value ratio is the major motivational factor for paying attention, especially for deep involvement or engagement of attention. Learning will not occur if the exhibit elements do not promise high enough value. Value is important during searching (visitors looking for something of value with which to engage).

How much potential value does an exhibit element have in the eyes of the visitor? Remember, value is a ratio of utility (benefit) divided by cost. Is the topic interesting? Does the visitor have time to invest in viewing the element? Is the perceived workload for engaging in the exhibit element too high?

PHYSICAL AND MENTAL STATES. There are a number of physical and mental states that can either increase or decrease the level of attention given to exhibitions and programs. These phenomena include physical and mental fatigue, energy level, object satiation, curiosity, and excitement. Museum design can help control many of these states. Reducing the physical and mental workload, encouraging rest periods (a café or places to rest), and making navigation as easy as possible so that visitors are not forced to spend time and energy wayfinding can all minimize fatigue. Varying the visitor experience so that visitors do not look at similar objects one after another can minimize object satiation. Varying the exhibit experience is important.

On the other hand, provoking curiosity and providing exciting discoveries for visitors can enhance the level of attention. Testing the impact of such visitor experiences (evaluation) is the only way to ensure that they really work. I have been involved with too many projects where the exhibition development committee believed that visitors would be blown away by something, but when tested, was disappointing.

STRATEGIES AND PATTERNS OF BEHAVIOR. Visitors employ a number of consistent patterns that are the result of past experiences and that enhance the visitor experience. For example, some seasoned museum-goers might first stop at the museum store to find more detailed information about the museum collection to better plan their visit. Some visitors might only read exhibit titles and ignore any other text. Parents with young children are more likely to read exhibit text and discuss exhibit content with their children. Reading habits (e.g., looking at the top element before the bottom element; starting at the left and proceeding to the right) also appear to influence how visitors distribute their attention within exhibits.

Between-Exhibit Considerations

When exhibit displays are placed together to form an exhibition, new potential problems occur (in addition to those that are common within an exhibit display). Do visitors bypass a less-interesting exhibit to stop at a more interesting one? Does a "landmark" object change the intended circulation

Table 16.1: Typical Problems and Solutions in Exhibition Design

PROBLEM	POSSIBLE SOLUTION
CAPTURE OF ATTENTION	
Visitors do not walk by exhibit or object	* Examine circulation flow * Consider simplifying route or adding wayfinding cues * Alter landmark attractors
Visitors turn the wrong way at an intersection or use only one path	* Create simpler system of pathways * Provide explicit direction cues
Visitors do not look at exhibit or object as they pass by	* Examine sight lines, proximity, salience of stimuli, and search process
Visitors look but do not approach, or do not stop	* Value may be low; examine time and effort necessary as well as interest level * Are there competing objects with higher value? * Consider using prompting device such as handouts or visitor guides
FOCUS OF ATTENTION	
Visitors only briefly focus on the exhibit element	* Look for distracting stimuli * Examine the value (benefit/cost)
Searching Sequence	
Visitors only focus on salient object but do not sequentially pay attention to the exhibit elements	* Examine layout of elements; is the sequence of moving from one element to another clear to visitor
ENGAGEMENT OF ATTENTION	
Visitors read very little of the interpretive material	* Value may be low (Text passages too long? Interest too low?) * Text poorly placed * Layout of exhibit elements may be confusing to visitors * High-value competing objects may be present
Visitors do not understand exhibit messages; did not learn what exhibit or exhibition is trying to teach	* Examine how much of the information is processed, how visitors are viewing the material, and the layout and wording of text material
Self-reports from visitors suggest material was difficult to understand, boring, or involved too much work to process	* Examine amount of content and how concisely it is presented, interest level, and layout of text material

flow of visitors as a result of visitors approaching the object? Do visitors move from one exhibit display to another in a manner that results in attention to all the important messages within the exhibition? Do visitors understand the intended traffic flow pattern? Do visual objects/elements compete for attention or do they complement one another?

1. **Sight lines.** The sight lines should flow easily so that visitors are encouraged to view exhibit displays in an orderly fashion.
2. **Layout or arrangement of exhibit displays.** The distance between displays and the layout (e.g., island versus wall placement) have strong implications for the distribution of visitor attention (Bitgood, Hines, Hamberger, & Ford 1991)

Common Problems and Solutions in Exhibition Design

The attention-value model provides a tool for both analyzing and solving potential problems (see Table 16.1). The table includes a number of problems that span the continuum of attention from capture to deep engagement. The list of these problems is not exhaustive. Hopefully, the list of problems and possible solutions provides a useful example of how the attention-value model can be applied to improving exhibition design.

There is no universal single solution to these problems. The attention-value model, however, does suggest what actions might be taken for specific problems at each stage of attention. The value ratio is important at every stage of attention. During the capture stage, detection of exhibit elements is likely to be a problem, and those factors associated with detection can be easily examined. Visitor circulation pathways and salience of exhibit elements should be assessed.

NOTES

1. There are many sources for exhibit evaluation. In addition to resources from the Visitor Studies Association and the American Alliance of Museums' Committee on Audience Research & Evaluation, the following references may be useful: Bitgood (1994; 1995), Bitgood & Shettel (1993, 1994), Miles (1993, 1994), Screven (1976, 1988, 1990), Shettel & Bitgood (1993), Shettel, Butcher, Cotton, Northrup, & Slough (1968), and Yalowitz & Bronnenkant (2009).
2. A resource and online community for informal learning projects, research, and evaluation can be found at http://Informalscience.org/

APPENDICES

A

Examples of Text Passages Used in the Simulation Studies

Georges Braque (1882–1963)

Musical Forms

The Philadelphia Museum of Art

- Braque, a major 20th century French painter, was born in 1882 and died in 1963.
- He tried several styles of art during his career, starting with Impressionism, then Fauvism, followed by a style similar to Cezanne, and finally Cubism.
- Braque shares with Picasso a pre-eminent position among cubist painters.
- This is no longer a "picture of" a violin, although a violin was the point of departure for some of its most conspicuous elements.
- Cubism developed so rapidly (around 1906 and 1907) that in retrospect, it seems to have been spontaneous.
- Picasso, Braque, and Juan Gris (among others) invented Cubism in that they all contributed to it and no one remembers who contributed which ideas.

Paul Cezanne (1839–1906)

Landscape with Viaduct

Metropolitan Museum of Art, New York

- This panoramic view is delicate and tranquil.
- The tree in the foreground is opposed to the distant landscape.
- We experience the vastness of the space in the broad valley with the viaduct and the mountains in the distance. The stream running down the center adds to the vastness of distance.
- The brushwork is legible and frank. It has many changes of direction and color.

- Cezanne is classified as a Post-Impressionist and is considered to be one of the forerunners of modern painters, partly because of his unique treatment of space, mass, and color.
- This artwork was completed in Cezanne's latter period in which he concentrated on still life, studies of bathers, and views/landscapes of Mount Sainte-Victoire.
- His work strongly influenced the Fauves, the Cubists, and most early 20th century art.

B

Checklist for Managing Visitor Attention

Checklist Rationale

1. Using the attention-value model, this checklist is designed to summarize and conceptually organize what we have learned about visitor attention.
2. The checklist attempts to identify the most important variables involved with visitor attention.
3. The checklist can also be used as an evaluation instrument to guide critical appraisals of exhibitions.

Cautions

1. To some extent, the relevance of these factors varies from exhibition to exhibition; in general, however, the same factors appear to influence visitor attention across types of exhibitions, types of museums, and types of visitors.
2. It is important to recognize the interplay between and among variables that influence visitor attention. Managing some of these variables (e.g., object size, topic interest, and/or layout of exhibit elements), but ignoring others (e.g., placement of objects with respect to other elements, to circulation pathway, and to line-of-sight location) is likely to lead to failure. If visitors do not easily notice an exhibit object, they are not likely to engage their attention to it.
3. For maximum benefit, the checklist requires a knowledgeable professional who possesses working experience with museum exhibitions. However, based on years of conducting hands-on workshops with museum professionals, I have found that professionals with even a little museum experience can benefit from application of the checklist.

Visitor Navigation

1. **Description-definition**

   a. **Conceptual orientation:** information describing what the exhibition is about, how it is organized, and what there is to see and do.

   b. **Physical orientation (wayfinding):** information that allows visitors to find their way in an efficient manner with minimal effort.

   c. **Circulation:** the interplay between the physical environment and user that influences how visitors move through exhibition spaces.

2. **Why is this important?** An effective system of orientation-circulation reduces the workload for visitors so they do not have to expend time and energy trying to understand the purpose, what to do, where to go, etc. An effective system also ensures that all exhibit elements are given a chance to be noticed. Often, the circulation pattern in exhibitions result in "hot" and "cold" spots with respect to visitor attention (e.g., Bitgood, et al., 1991). Differential attention to exhibit elements often occurs because of design that produces too much object competition or the necessity to backtrack in order to see all the elements.

3. **Conceptual orientation.** Does orientation communicate the main ideas and enough additional information to plan the visit?

   a. What is the exhibition all about? Does the title or a short statement communicate the main idea(s)?

   b. What is there to see and do? Does the orientation system effectively convey what the visitor will see and what can be done in the exhibition?

   c. How is it organized? Is there a graphic representation (i.e., a map) of how the exhibition is organized? Is the organization obvious from visual inspection?

   d. Is the placement, text length, size, etc. of text labels where it is needed?

4. **Wayfinding.** How much time and effort are required to navigate through the exhibition?

   a. **Wayfinding devices**

      1. Direction signs: Are direction signs placed in the location that they are needed (intersections)? Do they provide clear directions? Are they attention-getting?

      2. Maps: Are you-are-here (YAH) maps positioned where they are needed and do they follow the principles below?

3. Visitor guides: Do guides provide basic information (e.g., map of facility, what to do and see, where to find amenities) that visitors need to plan their visit and navigate?

b. **Guidelines for YAH maps**

1. Up on the map should be forward in the environment
2. Need two points of information, one on map that can be matched with one in the environment
3. YAH symbol
4. Simplicity (remove irrelevant information)

c. **Visual access.** Can the visitor see key locations (e.g., signage, objects) from the entrance of the exhibition?

Capturing Attention

1. **Description-definition.** When attention is captured, the visitor looks at, approaches, and/or stops at an exhibit element. Given the density and complexity of the exhibit environment, capturing attention in an orderly manner can be a challenge. When sound from an exhibit is also present, it contributes to its attracting power.

2. **Why is this important?** The first step in managing visitor attention to an exhibit element is the initial attraction. Obviously, without attraction of attention, an exhibit element has little value. One of the problems is to design the exhibit elements in a way that encourages systematic viewing of objects, text, etc. What attracts attention may also distract from attending to another exhibit element. Capturing attention is a juggling act: just as you must remember to keep all the objects simultaneously in the air without dropping any of them when you juggle, in an exhibition, the challenge is to juggle visitor attention to all the important elements without forgetting any of them.

3. **Salience/distinctiveness of exhibit elements.** How powerful are the exhibit elements in terms of their ability to capture attention?

a. **Size and scale:** which objects are large enough to capture attention?
b. **Movement:** is movement involved (e.g., living animals, moving parts, etc.)?
c. **Multisensory elements** (e.g., sound, touch)
d. **Isolation/density:** to what degree is the exhibit element isolated from other elements?

e. **Lighting:** how effective is lighting (focus, glare, light level for reading, etc.)?
f. **Line-of-sight:** are key exhibit elements within the visitor's line of sight?
g. **Figure-ground relations:** do the exhibit elements "pop out" of the background?

4. **Circulation** (Movement patterns through the exhibition increase or decrease chance of objects being viewed).
a. **Clarity and complexity of circulation route.**
1. **Clarity.** How clear is the circulation route or pathway through the exhibition?
2. **Complexity of layout** (square/rectangle, cloverleaf, figure-8, etc.). Factors that contribute to complexity include number of intersections or choice points, pathway geometry (straight, curved, etc.), and presence or absence of 90-degree intersections.
b. **Pathway**
1. Entrance and exits: are design of entrance and exits creating an "exit gradient"?
2. Pathways: are sub-pathways not likely to be used?
3. Do all exhibit displays have an equal chance of being viewed?
4. Is there universal, physical accessibility?
5. Proximity of elements to visitor (How closely to visitors circulate near elements? How does economy of movement relate to exhibition design?)
6. Landmarks: are landmark objects salient enough to influence visitor circulation?
7. Turning at intersections: is circulation path designed for economy of movement?
8. One-sided viewing: does the design encourage one-sided viewing?

Focusing Attention

1. **Description-definition.** Once attention is captured, the next concern is how and where the visitor focuses his/her attention. This is the process in which attention is briefly narrowed to a specific exhibit element. Which element and in what sequence become important questions. Designers use a number of techniques to help attention focusing. Examples of focusing methods include an instruction to "Look at . . . ." spotlighting

an object, using a sound associated with an exhibit element, isolating an object, or raising an object above others in a display case.

2. **Why is this important?** Once attention has been captured, the next step is to help visitors focus attention on relevant aspects of the exhibit elements and in a sequence that makes sense or is consistent with the intentions of the designers. If the exhibit elements are not designed with this in mind, visitors may be at a loss on how to distribute their attention or may visually explore in an inefficient manner or may just give up because it involves too much effort. "Value" (the combination of utility and costs) must be sufficient to keep attention focused enough for at least minimal impact to obtain focused attention.

3. **Perceptual factors**
   a. **Object competition:** do competing sights and sounds distract visitors?
   b. **Density of exhibit elements** (distance apart and total number of elements)
   c. **Distractions**
   d. **Competing sights and sounds**
      1. Attention-focusing devices
      2. Figure-ground: can text be easily distinguished from background (i.e., color differences)?

4. **Value (ratio of utility divided by cost)**
   a. **Utility** (perceived or actual benefit, satisfaction, etc.)
      1. Emotional-cognitive appeal
         · Provocative format (e.g., ask questions, confront misconceptions)
         · Friendly writing style
         · Immersion qualities (mental imagery, time-and-place)
         · Three-dimensional objects
      2. Inherent interest in subject matter

5. **Perceived and actual costs (time, effort, workload)**
   a. **Text length and number of labels**
   b. **Proximity of labels to objects**
   c. **Ease of processing information** (e.g., bulleting, concept map format)
   d. **Ease of searching** (e.g., number of distracters to scan?)
   e. **Physical accessibility:** size of fonts, distance from visitor, etc.

Engaging Attention

1. **Description-definition.** Engagement means that visitors become involved in exhibit content. This may mean reading text passages, thinking about content, discussing it with other group members, etc. Engagement is associated with learning and requires deeper processing and longer viewing time than the focus level of attention. When the visitor is engaged, attention is involved and committed to an exhibit element.

2. **Why is this important?** The most difficult task of exhibit design is to engage attention. Engagement requires deep processing of exhibit elements and longer viewing times. Engagement is necessary for communication, which can be explicit (use of language) or implicit (inferred from the presentation of the exhibit objects, organization and display techniques, etc.).

3. **Explicit communication**
   a. **Functions of written/verbal content**
      1. Instruct: focus attention: "Look at . . . ," or "Place your hands on the rectangles . . "
      2. Explain: tell what it means or why it is important
      3. Storyline
      4. Relevance: does message relate to objects/elements in exhibit? Do physical and verbal messages conflict with one another?
   b. **Value of content**
      1. High personal value and a relatively low cost required for visitor engagement
   c. **Characteristics of text passages and illustrations**
      1. Simplicity and length
      2. Clarity: are the exhibit messages clear to the visitor?
      3. Interest and personal relevance of object/content to visitor
      4. Nonverbal messages: consistency with verbal messages, cues to importance, etc.
      5. Are messages presented in a way that facilitates memory?
      6. Use of provocative "hooks" (e.g., "Can you identify the three animals in the totem pole?")
   d. **Characteristics of exhibit elements.** Does the organization/layout of exhibit elements appropriately relate to the verbal messages?
      1. Is there an obvious sequence of attending to elements: is it clear to visitors where to start?
      2. Is density of elements too high?

3. Design techniques reinforce the message (is importance of exhibit element communicated by lighting, isolation, etc.)
4. Is the organization clear to visitors?
5. Is it clear where one exhibit display ends and another begins?
6. Designed so that more than one individual can experience as a group?

4. **Implicit messages**
   a. **Techniques used to involve visitors**
      1. Immersion: creates feeling of time and place
      2. Realistic duplication of key elements
      3. Multisensory appropriate to a time and place
      4. Encouragement to mentally put oneself in time and place
   b. **Implicit messages associated with design**
      1. Relative size
      2. Object competition/isolation
      3. Relation of object to explicit messages

5. **Interactivity** (Principles for interactive devices)
   a. **Visibility:** By looking at the device, can the visitor determine what response is expected?
   b. **Feedback:** Do both correct and incorrect responses provide feedback to the visitor?
   c. **Instructions:** Are instructions minimal and placed where they are noticed and will be used?
   d. **Natural mapping:** Are controls mapped out in a similar pattern as what is being controlled?
   e. **Explanation:** Is the explanation concise, clear, and separated from instructions?

6. **Audiovisual (AV) presentation**
   a. Is it short enough to sustain attention?
   b. Does the content provide sufficient information, but not create overload?
   c. Does the AV fit well with the main messages of the exhibition?
   d. Is the AV isolated from competing exhibit elements?
   e. Is there a synopsis of the AV and information about length and when it starts?
   f. Is seating provided if it is more than 15 to 20 seconds in length?

g. Is the visitor asked to show commitment, such as pay a fee, wait in line, etc.?

NOTE: Each exhibit display may need to be assessed using the above criteria: attracting, holding, and communication power. General statements about the entire exhibition are less useful for diagnostic purposes than reference to specific elements.

Other Factors To Consider

1. **Comfort**
   a. Are there places to rest?
   b. Is the temperature and lighting comfortable?
   c. Is sound level comfortable?
   d. Is the exhibition designed to pace visitors to minimize "fatigue"?

2. **Safety**
   a. Are there any safety issues with children or visitors of other ages?
   b. Can children climb on exhibit elements?
   c. Are there sharp corners or other dangerous features of exhibit elements?
   d. Do live animals pose a safety threat?

3. **Satisfaction, curiosity, interest**
   a. Are the topics of high interest to visitors?
   b. Does the exhibition stimulate visitor curiosity?
   c. Does the experience create satisfaction?
   d. Is there a sense of discovery, such as seeing things in a new way or learning something new?
   e. Does the exhibit create empathy (feelings aroused for others such as victims of natural disaster or discrimination)?
   f. Is there a feeling of being in the time and place?
   g. Does the entertainment value overpower the educational goals of the exhibit element?

References

Adelman, L., Falk, J., & James, S. (2000). Impact of National Aquarium in Baltimore on visitors' conservation attitudes, behavior, and knowledge. *Curator,* 43(1), 33–61.

Ainley, M., Hidi, S., & Berndorff, D. (2002). Interest, learning, and the psychological processes that mediate their relationship. *Journal of Educational Psychology,* 94(3), 545–561.

Allen, S., & Gutwill, J. (2009). Creating a program to deepen family inquiry at interactive science exhibits. *Curator,* 52(3), 289–306.

Arkes, H., & Blumer, C. (1985). The psychology of sunk costs. *Organizational Behavior and Human Decision Making,* 35, 124–140.

Ashcraft, M, & Radvansky, G. (2010). *Cognition (5th edition).* Upper Saddle River, NJ: Prentiss Hall.

Bickford, A. (2010). Review of *Identity and the Museum Visitor Experience. Curator,* 53(2), 247–255.

Birney, B. (1990). Using rotating guides to interpret immersion exhibits: A solution to public display problems. In *Current Trends in Audience Research and Evaluation.* Chicago, IL: AAM Visitor Research and Evaluation Committee, pp. 1–3.

Bitgood, S. (1989). Deadly sins revisited: A review of the exhibit label literature. *Visitor Behavior,* 4(3), 4–11.

_____. (1991). Simulated immersion. Technical Report No. 91-10, Jacksonville, AL: Center for Social Design.

_____. (1994). Classification of exhibit evaluation: How deep should Occam's Razor cut? *Visitor Behavior,* 9(3), 8–10.

_____. (1995). Remedial evaluation: Definition, issues, and implementation. In *Museen und ihre Besucher.* Bonn, Germany: Haus der Geschichte *der Bundesrepublik Deutschland,* pp. 49–59.

_____. (2000). The role of attention in the designing effective interpretive labels. *Journal of Interpretation Research,* 5(2), 31–45.

_____. (2002). Environmental psychology in museums, zoos, and other exhibition centers. In *Handbook of environmental psychology,* R. Bechtel & A. Churchman (eds.). New York, NY: John Wiley & Sons, pp. 461–480.

_____. (2003). Visitor orientation: Are museums similar to casinos? *Visitor Studies Today,* 6(1), 10–12. (Also in Bitgood, S. (2011). *Social design in museums: The psychology of visitor studies.* Edinburgh, UK: MuseumsEtc., pp. 418–426.)

_____. (2006). An analysis of visitor circulation: Movement patterns and the general value principle. *Curator,* 49, 463–475.

_____. (2009a). When is "museum fatigue" not fatigue? *Curator,* 52(2), 193–202.

_____. (2009b). Museum fatigue: A critical review. *Visitor Studies,* 12(2), 93–111.

Bitgood, S. (2009c). Museum fatigue: A new look at an old problem. *Informal Learning Review,* 97 (July-August).

_____. (2010). *An attention-value model of museum visitors.* The Center for the Advancement of Informal Science Education. Available at http://caise.insci.org/uploads/docs/VSA_Bitgood.pdf.

_____. (2011a). *Social design in museums: The psychology of visitor studies, Vols. 1 and 2.* Edinburgh, UK: MuseumsEtc.

_____. (2011b). A comparison of formal and informal learning. In S. Bitgood, *Social design in museums: The psychology of visitor studies, Vol. 1.* Edinburgh, UK: MuseumsEtc., pp. 90–109.

_____. (2011c). Immersion experiences in museums. In S. Bitgood, *Social design in museums: The psychology of visitor studies, Vol. 2.* Edinburgh, UK: MuseumsEtc., pp. 105–121.

Bitgood, S., Benefield, A., & Patterson, D. (1987). *Evaluation of orientation at the Space & Rocket Center.* Unpublished Report. Jacksonville, AL: Psychology Institute, Jacksonville State University.

Bitgood, S., Benefield, A., Patterson, D., & Litwak, H. (1992). Visitor attention and life-sized animal silhouettes. In *Visitor studies: Theory, research, and practice, Vol. 3,* S. Bitgood, A. Benefield, & D. Patterson (eds.). Jacksonville, AL: Center for Social Design, pp. 221–230.

Bitgood, S., Burt, R., & Dukes, S. (2009). An examination of multiple measures of "museum fatigue." Presented at Southern Society for Philosophy and Psychology, Savannah, GA, April 9–11.

_____. (2010). Effects of perceptual distraction, choice, and persistence on attention. Presented at the Visitor Studies Conference, Phoenix, AZ, July 29–31.

Bitgood, S., Cleghorn, A., Cota, A., Crawford, M., Patterson, D., & Danemeyer, C. (1996). Enhancing the Confrontation Gallery at the Birmingham Civil Rights Institute. *Visitor Studies: Theory, Research, & Practice* 7(1), 49–56.

Bitgood, S., Conroy, P., Pierce, M., Patterson, D., & Boyd, J. (1989). Evaluation of attract and defense at the Anniston Museum of Natural History. In *Current Trends in Audience Research and Evaluation, Vol. 3.* New Orleans, LA: AAM Committee on Audience Research and Evaluation, pp. 1–4.

Bitgood, S., Davey, G., Huang, X., & Fung, H. (In Press). Pedestrian choice behavior at shopping mall intersections in China and the United States. *Environment & Behavior.* Prepublished online July 17, 2012, DOI: 0013916512450172.

Bitgood, S., & Davis, J. (1992). Self-guided handouts in museums and zoos: An annotated bibliography. *Visitor Behavior,* 6(3), 7–10.

Bitgood, S., C. Devia, P. Goodwin, C. Rudin, A. Trammell, & Zimmerman, B. (2001). Projective focusing: Motivated attention to works of art. *Current Trends in Audience Research Vol. 14.* St. Louis, MO: AAM Committee on Audience Research and Evaluation, pp. 25–31.

Bitgood, S., & Dukes, S. (2006). Not another step! Economy of movement and pedestrian choice point behavior in shopping malls. *Environment and Behavior,* 38, 394–405.

Bitgood, S., & Dukes, S. (2011). Choosing to read when quality of information and amount of effort vary simultaneously. In *Social design in museums: The psychology of visitor studies,* S. Bitgood (ed.). Edinburgh, UK: MuseumsEtc., pp. 280–282.

Bitgood, S., Dukes, S., & Abby, L. (2007). Interest and effort as predictors of reading: A test of the general value principle. *Current Trends in Audience Research and Evaluation Vol. 19/20.* Boston, MA: AAM Committee on Audience Research and Evaluation, pp. 5–10.

Bitgood, S., Dukes, S., & New, B. (2006). The role of value, interest, and effort on reading text. Paper presented at the Annual Meeting of the Southern Society of Psychology & Philosophy, Charleston, SC, April 13–15.

Bitgood, S., Hines, J., Hamberger, W., & Ford, W. (1991). A study of visitor circulation through five changing exhibitions. In *Visitor studies: Theory, research and practice, Vol. 4,* A. Benefield, S. Bitgood, & H. Shettel (eds.). Jacksonville, AL: Center for Social Design, pp. 103–114.

Bitgood, S., McKerchar, T., & Dukes, S. (In press). Melton's study of gallery density and visitor attention: Perceptual distraction or choice? *Visitor Studies.*

Bitgood, S., & New, B. (2012). *Visual search patterns in visitors.* Unpublished manuscript. Jacksonville, AL: Jacksonville State University.

Bitgood, S., New, B., & Abby, L. (2011). Viewing time of films: Why visitors do not view long films in museums. In *Social design in museums: The psychology of visitor studies, Vol. 1,* Bitgood, S. (ed.). Edinburgh, UK: MuseumsEtc., pp. 277–279.

Bitgood, S., New, B., & White, K. (2008). Projective focusing, engaged attention, and value: How do they relate to interest and reading? Paper presented at the Annual Meeting of the Southern Society of Philosophy & Psychology, New Orleans, LA, March 20–22.

Bitgood, S., Nichols, G., Pierce, M., Conroy, P., & Patterson, D. (1986). *Effect of label characteristics on visitor behavior.* Technical Report No. 86-55. Jacksonville, AL: Center for Social Design.

Bitgood, S., & Patterson, D. (1987). Visitor orientation at the Anniston Museum of Natural History. *Visitor Behavior,* 1(4), 6.

Bitgood, S., Patterson, D., & Benefield, A. (1986). Understanding your visitors: Ten factors that influence visitor behavior. *American Association of Zoological Parks and Aquaria Annual Conference Proceedings,* Minneapolis, MN, pp. 726–743.

_____. (1988). Exhibit design and visitor behavior: Empirical relationships. *Environment and Behavior,* 20(4), 474–491.

Bitgood, S., & Richardson, K. (1987). Wayfinding at the Birmingham Zoo. *Visitor Behavior,* 1(4), 9. (Also in S. Bitgood, (2011), Social design in museums: The psychology of visitor studies. Edinburgh, UK: MuseumsEtc., pp. 344–347.)

Bitgood, S., & Shettel, H. (1993). Exhibit/program evaluation: A participatory workshop. *Karlsruher Schriften zur Besucherforschung.* Heft, 4, 3–19. [Zum forschungstand der vorabelevaluation.]

_____. (1994). The classification of evaluation: A rationale for remedial evaluation. *Visitor Behavior,* 9(1), 4–8.

Bitgood, S., & Tisdal, C. (1996). Does lobby orientation influence visitor satisfaction? *Visitor Behavior,* 11(3), 13–16. (Also in Bitgood, S. (2011). *Social design in museums: The psychology of visitor studies, Vol. 1.* Edinburgh, UK: MuseumsEtc., pp. 408–417.)

Borun, M. (1977). *Measuring the Immeasurable: A Pilot Study of Museum Effectiveness.* Philadelphia, PA: Franklin Institute.

______. (1990). Naive notions and the design of science museum exhibits. In *Visitor studies: Theory, research and practice, Vol. 2,* S. Bitgood, A. Benefield, & D. Patterson (eds.). Jacksonville, AL: Center for Social Design, pp. 158–162.

Borun, M., Chambers, M., & Cleghorn, A. (1996). Families are learning in science museums. *Curator,* 39(2), 123–138.

Borun, M., Chambers, M., Dritsas, J. & Johnson, J. (1997). Enhancing family learning through exhibits. *Curator,* 40(4), 279–295.

Borun, M., & Dtitsas, J. (1997). Devleoping family-friendly exhibits. *Curator,* 40(3), 178–196.

Borun, M., & Miller, M. (1980). To label or not to label? *Museum News,* 58(4), 64–67.

Briseño-Garzon, A., Anderson, D., & Anderson, A. (2007). Entry and emergent agendas of adult visiting in aquarium in family groups. *Visitor Studies,* 10(1), 73–89.

Canaday, J. (1958). *Metropolitan Seminars in Art Series.* New York: Metropolitan Museum of Art.

Carlson, S. (1993). Cognitive model for learning in educationally oriented recreation facilities [Ph.D. dissertation]. Department of Park and Recreational Resources, Michigan State University, East Lansing.

Chambers, M. (1990). Improving the Aesthetic Experience for Art Novices: A New Paradigm for Interpretive Labels. In *The Denver Art Museum Interpretive Project,* M. McDermott-Lewis (ed.). Denver, CO: Denver Art Museum, pp. 101–110.

Chambers, M., & Muir, H. (1990). Learning to Look: A Coaching Brochure for Art Novices. In *The Denver Art Museum Interpretive Project,* M. McDermott-Lewis (ed.). Denver, CO: Denver Art Museum, pp. 111–120.

Coe, J. (1986). Towards a co-evolution of zoos, aquariums, and natural history museums. *AAZPA 1986 Conference Proceedings.* Minneapolis, MN: American Association of Zoological Parks & Aquariums.

Corbetta, M., & Shulman, G. (2002). Control of goal-directed and stimulus-driven attention in the brain. *Nature Reviews Neuroscience,* 3, 201–215.

Critchfield, T., & Kollins, S. (2001). Temporal discounting: Basic research and the analysis of socially important behavior. *Journal of Applied Behavior Analysis,* 34(1), 101–122.

Csikszentmihalyi, M. (1990). *Flow: The psychology of optimal experience.* New York: Harper & Row.

Dawson, E., & Jensen, E. (2011). Towards a "contextual turn" in visitor studies: Evaluating visitor segmentation and identity-related motivations. *Visitor Studies,* 14(2), 127–140.

DeWaard, R. J., Jagmin, N., Maistro, S. A., & McNamara, P. A. (1974). Effects of Using Programmed Cards on Learning in a Museum Environment. *Journal of Educational Research,* 67(10), 457–460.

Du Toit, H., & Dye, B. (2008). Empathic dramatic engagement as a metaphor for learning in the art museum. *Visitor Studies,* 11(1), 73–89.

Eisenberger, R. (1985). Learned industriousness. *Psychological Review,* 99(2), 248–267.

Ellis, J. (1993). Learning from museum exhibits: The influence of sequence, verbal ability, field dependence, and perspective-taking instructions [Ph.D. dissertation]. College of Education, University of Florida, Gainsville, FL.

Falk, J., & Dierking, L. (1992). *The museum experience.* Walnut Creek, CA: Left Coast Press.

_____. (2000). *Learning from museums: visitor experiences and the making of meaning.* Lanham, MD: AltaMira Press.

_____. (2012). *The museum experience revisited.* Walnut Creek, CA: Left Coast Press.

Falk, J., Moussouri, T., & Coulson, D. (1998). The effect of visitors' agendas on museum learning. *Curator,* 41(2), 107–119.

Frechtling, Joy (2010). The 2010 User-Friendly Handbook for Project Evaluation. December 2010. Available at http://informalscience.org/downloads/TheUserFriendlyGuide.pdf.

Frederick, S., Loewenstein, G., & O'Donoghue, T. (2002). Time discounting and time preference: A critical review. *Journal of Economic Literature,* 40(2) (June 2002), 351–401.

Fry, H. (1987). Worksheets as museum learning devices. *Museums Journal,* 86(4), 219–225.

Gilman, B. (1916). Museum fatigue. *Scientific Monthly,* 12, 67–74.

Goldfarb, R., & Ratner, J. (2008). "Theory" and "models": Terminology through the looking glass. *Econ Journal Watch,* 5(1), 91–108.

Green, L., & Myerson, J. (2004). A discounting framework for choice with delayed and probabilistic rewards. *Psychological Bulletin,* 130(5), 769–792.

Gyllenhaal, E. (2002). Immersive exhibitions: A bibliography. *Visitor Studies Today,* 5(3), 13–14.

Harvey, M., Loomis, R., Bell, P., & Marino, M. (1998). The influence of museum exhibit design on immersion and psychological flow. *Environment and Behavior,* 30(5), 601–627.

Hein, G. (1998). *Learning in the museum.* London: Routledge.

Howes, D. S. (1990). Wayfinding at the Art Institute of Chicago. In *Current Trends in Audience Research and Evaluation.* Chicago, IL: AAM Visitor Evaluation and Research Committee, pp. 5–10.

James, W. (1890). *Principles of psychology.* Cambridge, MA: Harvard University Press.

Kahneman, D., & Tversky, A. (1979). Prospect theory: An analysis of decision under risk. *Econometrica,* 47(2), 263–292.

Kaplan, S. (1983). A model of person-environment compatibility. *Environment and Behavior,* 15, 311–332.

Kaplan, S., Bardwell, L., & Slakter, D. (1993). The museum as a restorative environment. *Environment and Behavior,* 25(6), 725–742.

Kaplan, R., & Kaplan, S. (1989). *The experience of nature: A psychological perspective.* New York: Cambridge University Press.

Kivetz, R. (2003). The effects of effort and intrinsic motivation on risky choice. *Marketing Science,* 22(4), 477–502.

Koran, J., & Koran, M. (1983). The role of attention and curiosity in museum learning. *Journal of Museum Education,* 8(2), 14–17.

_____. (1986a). A proposed framework for exploring museum education research. *Museum Education Roundtable,* 11(1), 95–99.

_____. (1986b). The roles of attention and curiosity in museum learning. *Museum Education Roundtable,* 8(2), 14–17.

Koran, J., Koran, M., & Foster, J. (1988). Individual differences in learning in informal settings. In *Visitor studies: Theory, research, and practice. Vol. 1,* S. Bitgood, J. Roper, & A. Benefield (eds.), pp. 66–72.

_____. (1989). The potential contributions of cognitive psychology to visitor studies. In *Visitor studies: Theory, research, and practice. Vol. 2,* S. Bitgood, A. Benefield (eds.), pp. 74–80.

Korn, R. (1988). Self-guiding brochures: An evaluation. *Curator,* 31(1), 9–19.

Krapp, A., & Prenzel, M. (2011). Research on interest in science: Theories, methods, and findings. *International Journal of Science Education,* 33(1), 27–50.

Krulick, J. & Ritchie, M. (1990). Expanding the novice experience. In *The Denver Art Museum Interpretive Project,* M. McDermott-Lewis (ed.). Denver, CO: Denver Art Museum, pp. 49–54.

Lakota, R. (1975). *The National Museum of Natural History as a behavioral environment: Part 1: An environmental analysis of behavioral performance.* Washington, DC: Office of Museum Programs, Smithsonian Institution.

Langer, E. (1989). *Mindfulness.* Reading, MA: Addison Wesley.

LeClaire, L., & Grabski, V. (2010). *Gallery guides in the Tete-a-Tete Exhibit.* Frye Art Museum, Seattle, WA.

Levine, M. (1982). You-are-here maps: Guiding principles. *Environment and Behavior,* 14(2), 221–237.

Lightner, J. (1998). An attention model for museum exhibits [Ph.D. dissertation]. College of Education, Lansing, MI: Michigan State University.

Linnenbrink-Garcia, L., Durik, A., Conley, A. Barron, K., Tauer, J., Karabenick, S., & Haracckiewicz, J. (2010). Measuring situational interest in academic domains. *Educational and Psychological Measurement,* 20(10), 1–25.

Loomis, R. (1982). Evaluation of a visitor gallery guide. *The Visitor and the Denver Art Museum Working Report, No. 2.*

Matamoros, M. (1986). Information overload [Master's thesis]. Department of Management, University of Massachusetts at Boston, Boston, MA.

McManus, P. M. (1985). Worksheet-induced behaviour in the British Museum (Natural History). *Journal of Biological Education,* 19(3), 237–242.

Melton, A. (1935). *Problems of installation in museums of art.* New Series No. 14. Washington, DC: American Association of Museums.

_____. (1972). Visitor behavior in museums: Some early research in environmental design. *Human Factors,* 14(5), 393–403.

Melton, A., Feldman, N., & Mason, C. (1936). *Experimental studies of the education of children in a museum of science.* New Series No. 15. Washington, DC: American Association of Museums.

Miles, R. S. (1993). Grasping the greased pig: Evaluation of educational exhibits. In *Museum Visitor Studies in the 1990s,* S. Bicknell & G. Farmelo (eds.). London: Science Museum of London, pp. 24–33.

_____. (1994). Let's hear it for Mr. Occam: A reply to Bitgood & Shettel on remedial evaluation. *Visitor Behavior,* 9(3), 4–7.

Moscardo, G. (1999). *Making visitors mindful: Principles for creating quality sustainable visitor experiences through effective communication.* Champaign, IL: Sagamore Publishing.

National Park Service (2003). *Visitor use and evaluation of interpretive media.* A Report on Visitors to the National Park Service. Social Science Program.

Packer, J. (2008). Beyond learning: Exploring visitors' perceptions of the value and benefits of museum experiences. *Curator,* 51(1), 33–54.

Perry, D. (1993). Measuring learning with the knowledge hierarchy. In *Visitor studies: Theory, research, and practice, Vol. 6,* D. Thompson, S. Bitgood, A. Benefield, H. Shettel, & R. Williams (eds). Jacksonville, AL: Visitor Studies Association, pp. 73–77.

_____. (2012). *What makes learning fun? Principles for the design of intrinsically motivating museum exhibits.* Lanham, MD: AltaMira Press.

Pirolli, P., & Card, S. (1999). Information foraging. *Psychological Review,* 106(4), 643–675.

Porter, M. (1938). *Behavior of the Average Visitor in the Peabody Museum of Natural History Yale University.* New Series No. 16. Washington, DC: American Association of Museums.

Posner, M., & Cohen, Y. (1984). Components of visual attention. In *Attention and performance,* H. Bouma & D. G. Bouhuis (eds.). Hillsdale, NJ: Erlbaum, pp. 531–556.

Rachlin, H., & Green, L. (1972). Commitment, choice and self-control. *Journal of the Experimental Anaylsis of Behavior,* 17, 15–22.

Rand, J. (1985). Fish stories that hook readers: Interpretive graphics at the Monterey Bay Aquarium. Columbus, OH: 1985 *AAZPA Annual Proceedings,* pp. 404–413.

Robinson, E. (1928). *The behavior of the museum visitor.* New Series No. 5. Washington, DC: American Association of Museums.

Rounds, J. (2004). Strategies for the curiosity-driven museum visitor. *Curator,* 47(4), 389–410.

Rowe, S., & Nickels, A. (2011). Visitor motivations across three informal education institutions: An application of the identity-related visitor motivation model. *Visitor Studies,* 14(2), 162–175.

Russell, R. (2000). Designing exhibits that engage visitors: Bob's top ten points. The *Informal Learning Review,* No. 45, Nov./Dec.

Screven, C. G. (1975). The effectiveness of guidance devices on visitor learning. *Curator,* 18(3), 219–243.

_____. (1976). Exhibit evaluation: A goal-referenced approach. *Curator,* 19(4), 271–290.

_____. (1986). Exhibitions and information centers: Some principles and approaches. *Curator,* 29(2), 109–137.

_____. (1988). Formative evaluation: Conceptions and misconceptions. In *Visitor studies–1988: Theory, research, and practice. Proceedings of the first annual Visitor Studies Conference,* S. Bitgood, J. Roper, & A. Benefield (eds.). Jacksonville, AL: Center for Social Design, pp. 73–82.

_____. (1990). Uses of evaluation before, during, and after exhibit design. *ILVS Review: A Journal of Visitor Behavior,* 1(2), 36–66.

_____. (1992). Motivating visitors to read labels. *ILVS Review: A Journal of Visitor Behavior,* 2(2), 183–211.

_____. (1999). Information design in informal settings: Museums and other public places. In *Information design,* R. Jacobson (ed.). Cambridge, MA: MIT Press, pp. 131–192.

Sedlmaier, J. J. (2012) The motion-graphic ads of Burma-Shave: 1927-1963. Imprint, May 8. Available at http://imprint.printmag.com/branding/the-morbid-roadside-ad-poetry-of-burma-shave/.

Serrell, B. (1983). *Making exhibit labels: A step by step guide.* Nashville, TN: American Association for State and Local History.

_____. (1996). *Exhibit labels: An interpretive approach.* Lanham, MD: AltaMira Press.

_____. (1998). *Paying attention: Visitors and museum exhibitions.* Washington, DC: American Association of Museums.

_____. (2002). Are they watching? Visitors and videos in exhibitions. *Curator,* 45(1), 50–64.

Shettel, H., & Bitgood, S. (1993). Les pratiques de l'évaluation des expositions [The practical use of exhibit evaluation]. *Publics et Musees,* 4, 9–25.

Shettel, H., Butcher, M., Cotton, T., Northrup, J., & Slough, D. (1968). *Strategies for determining exhibit effectiveness.* Report AIR-E95-4/68-FR. Pittsburgh: American Institutes for Research.

Simon, H. A. (1956). Rational choice and the structure of the environment. *Psychological Review,* 63(2), 129–138.

Spilkova, J., & Hochel, M. (2009). Toward an economy of pedestrian movement in Czech and Slovak shopping malls. *Environment and Behavior,* 41, 443–455.

Thompson, D., & Bitgood, S. (1988). The effects of sign length, letter size, and proximity on reading. In *Visitor studies–1988: Theory, research, and practice,* S. Bitgood, J. Roper, & A. Benefield (eds.). Jacksonville, AL: Center for Social Design, pp. 101–112.

Vocabulary Vocabulary (2007). "Prompting." Available at http://vocabulary-vocabulary.com/dictionary/prompting.php.

Wilkinson, N. (2008). *An introduction to behavioral economics.* New York: Palgrave Macmillan.

Worts, D. (1989). Shaking the foundations: Recent audience research at the Art Gallery of Ontario. In *Visitor studies: Theory, research and practice, Vol. 2,* S. Bitgood, A. Benefield, & D. Patterson (eds.). Jacksonville, AL: Center for Social Design, pp. 203–210.

_____. (1993). Gallery enhancement: Forging a new partnership with the public. In *Visitor studies: Theory, research, and practice, Vol. 6,* D. Thompson, S. Bitgood, A. Benefield, H. Shettel, & R. Williams (eds.). Jacksonville, AL: Center for Social Design, pp. 176–197.

Yalowitz, S., & Bronnenkant, K. (2009). Timing and tracking: Unlocking visitor behavior. *Visitor Studies,* 12(1), 47–64.

Yellis, K. (1990). *Real time: The theory and practice of living history at Plimoth Plantation.* Unpublished manuscript, Plymouth, MA.

Index

M

N

O

P

About the Author

Stephen Bitgood, Ph.D., is Professor Emeritus in the Department of Psychology at Jacksonville State University in Alabama. After several years of work in experimental, clinical, and educational psychology, he began studying visitors in museums, parks, and zoos in 1984. He has traveled extensively conducting research with visitors, evaluating exhibitions, conducting workshops for professionals, and presenting conference papers. His work has focused on applying a scientific, psychological approach to the study of visitors; his wide-ranging publications in visitor studies include *Social Design in Museums: The Psychology of Visitor Studies* (MuseumsEtc, 2011), a chapter in the *Handbook of Environmental Psychology* (Bechtel & Churchman, 2002), and articles in *Visitor Studies*, *Visitor Studies Today*, *Curator*, *Journal of Interpretation Research*, and *Journal of Museum Education*, among many others.

green press INITIATIVE

Left Coast Press, Inc. is committed to preserving ancient forests and natural resources. We elected to print this title on 30% post consumer recycled paper, processed chlorine free. As a result, for this printing, we have saved:

3 Trees (40' tall and 6-8" diameter)
2 Million BTUs of Total Energy
280 Pounds of Greenhouse Gases
1,519 Gallons of Wastewater
102 Pounds of Solid Waste

Left Coast Press, Inc. made this paper choice because our printer, Thomson-Shore, Inc., is a member of Green Press Initiative, a nonprofit program dedicated to supporting authors, publishers, and suppliers in their efforts to reduce their use of fiber obtained from endangered forests.

For more information, visit www.greenpressinitiative.org

Environmental impact estimates were made using the Environmental Defense Paper Calculator. For more information visit: www.papercalculator.org.